# Measuring Spiritual Maturity

## A Process to Move People from Spiritual Babies to Spiritual Adults

### Dr. Randy Tompkins

ISBN 978-1-64569-509-7 (paperback)
ISBN 978-1-64569-510-3 (digital)

Christian Faith Publishing, Inc.
832 Park Avenue
Meadville, PA 16335
www.christianfaithpublishing.com

Printed in the United States of America

# CONTENTS

# PREFACE

*A* disciple-making process is not a one-step process. Many facets of a quality disciple-making process exist: prayer, Bible reading, community, stewardship, sharing your faith, belief about God, belief about Jesus, belief about the Bible, belief about baptism, belief about worship, serving in church ministries, and a measurement tool to measure each of these facets.

I was born into a Christian environment a few years after War World II. Herbert Springer Tompkins was my father, and Rachel Ellaine Smith Tompkins was my mother. Both of my parents were born to Christian parents. My maternal grandfather was a circuit-riding preacher in Tennessee. I have never known a time when my parents and grandparents were not active in church. To our family, the Bible was not just a book to be placed on the coffee table, it was a book used to guide the family.

At the age of seven, I walked into the living room of our house and announced to my parents that I wanted to be saved. I can still remember the joy that overcame them as we began our discussion. My father asked me several questions that I answered as best I could using sentences and words I had heard in Sunday School. After we had prayer, I returned to my bedroom. A little while later, I returned to the living room and announced I just wanted to see what being saved felt like. In a matter of a few moments, my parents' emotions went from confusion to sadness to loving parents.

At the age of ten I was attending my final Vacation Bible School as a student. I thought I was going to be too big for VBS the following year, so I announced to my parents this would be my last year. All week I had thoughts going through my mind about God, Jesus, church, and what it all meant. On Thursday morning we conducted the daily opening VBS exercise. At the conclusion of the exercise, our pastor gave an altar call and two of my friends went forward.

I remained standing at my chair, firmly gripping the chair back in front of me. I had a feeling I needed to respond but did not want to.

After a few minutes we were dismissed and went to our classrooms. When I entered our room, I grabbed the first chair that was vacant. It also happened to be the chair closest to the door. I scooted the chair away from the wall and leaned back on the back two legs of the chair and began to think. To this day I do not remember what was happening around me. I was thinking through all the questions I had been dodging during the week.

At that moment, the door opened slowly, and my mother looked around the edge of the door. She saw me and simply whispered, "Randy, don't you think it's time?" And that was all she was able to say. I jumped up and ran to the fellowship hall building, where our pastor was counseling two of my friends. When Reverend Nolan asked why I had come to the room, I simply replied that I wanted to be saved. That day Jimmy, Gary, and I truly accepted Jesus as our Savior.

From that point until I was beyond thirty years of age, I continually tried to follow what I thought God was leading me to do. However, during that time, no one helped me understand what it meant to grow spiritually. The general opinion was if I attended church and Sunday school regularly and read my Bible, I would grow spiritually. While those steps will assist the spiritual growth, there is more to spiritual growth. The only direction given to church members about spiritual growth in the 1960s revolved around evangelism. I was doing everything other people were telling me I needed to do in order to grow my Christian faith, but I didn't feel true spiritual growth.

After being a church staff minister for almost twenty years, God led me to become a part of the Mississippi Baptist Convention Board Sunday School Department. One of my responsibilities was to develop and produce Sunday school training material. During the next eight years, I gradually became aware of the fact spiritual growth is more than being saved, listening to Bible lessons, and attending church. These three things are very important but are only a part of the steps a person should take in order to experience spiritual growth.

God then led me to the Louisiana Baptist Convention to be the state Sunday School Director. As Sunday school director, I became increasingly aware that Sunday school teachers should do more to help students experience spiritual growth. At age sixty-six I was accepted into the doctoral program at Midwestern Baptist Theological Seminary. During the final seminar of my doctoral program, the dean of the program announced we were to come the next day with the title we would each use for our dissertation. Through the entire process of participating in the various seminars, I maintained I would write about the concept of various teaching methods.

The next day, Dr. Harrison started calling on people to give the title they had selected. Four of the first six people to respond presented a title dealing with teaching styles, techniques, etc. When it was my turn to state my title, the words "Measuring Spiritual Maturity" came out of my mouth. I was more stunned that anyone else in the room. Then the questions began to swirl in my mind: Where did that title come from? How was I going to research this topic? Could I write the required number of pages about this topic?

After everyone in the class had declared a title, Dr. Harrison said in two days each of us would give a fifteen-minute PowerPoint presentation about our title, followed by five minutes of questions from class members and comments from Dr. Harrison. This assignment brought forth a new set of questions.

Following supper, I returned to the hotel room and began thinking how I was going to put all this together. I did spend time praying and calling on God to give me direction. During the prayer time, I had the sensation God was reminding me He had been preparing me for this assignment for several decades. As I sat at the desk to sketch an outline for the PowerPoint, various ideas, resources, and questions came to mind. The concept for the contents of this book was born from the PowerPoint presented in class.

This book is designed to allow readers to examine one of many approaches to disciple-making. Several statements throughout the book give readers permission to alter the process to fit each church. The adage of "One size fits all" does not necessarily apply to disciple-making. The only thing I ask is to be careful in the customization. It is one thing to alter a program to fit the size, theology, and personality of a church; however, it is another thing to delete something because of personal preferences.

Research for this topic was started with a general search on the Internet for spiritual-growth surveys. This was not intended to be a scientific search. It was the fastest way to identify what spiritual inventories were available, which would be followed by detailed and serious research before the writing could start. The search on the Internet resulted in finding 14,000 titles of material relating to spiritual surveys. Not all of the surveys were studied, but 200 of them were closely examined.

Two things were learned from the examination. First, documents and programs exist on the Internet with the term *spiritual growth* in the titles that have nothing to do with spiritual growth or spiritual-growth surveys. Secondly, most of the programs that were examined were duplications of other spiritual-growth programs. Fourteen spiritual-growth surveys were identified as having some element of distinction from the other 186. These surveys are listed in appendix B.

The main information for Measuring Spiritual Maturity is found in chapters 5, 6, and 7 and appendix C. However, the background for the process is found in chapters 1–4 and 8.

My prayer is the information in this book will be beneficial both to individuals and entire church congregations.

# CHAPTER 1

## Developing Measuring Spiritual Maturity Material

$T$he Measuring Spiritual Maturity material was developed with a specific purpose to give the church a viable tool to see the spiritual growth of members of the congregation. The first part of the development journey was to determine the availability of spiritual-growth material to the church. Cornerstone Consultants conducted research to find spiritual assessment material. More than 1,400 spiritual-growth inventories were found through an Internet search. Most of the material was eliminated due to repetition or a lack of substantive material. Fourteen spiritual-growth assessments were found to be different from the rest of the discovered assessments.

Twelve of the fourteen assessments were developed for individual use. These assessments were designed for a one-time administration to be either self-administered and scored or administered by a friend who would also score the assessment. Speculation about spiritual growth was implied by written instructions when the assessment was scored. However, since the assessment was to be administered only one time, it would be difficult to measure spiritual growth. A one-time administration would only provide a snapshot of the spiritual state of the individual at the time of the completion of the assessment.

The other two assessments were developed to be used by groups of people. One assessment was designed to be used by groups of people within an individual church. The second assessment was designed to be used by groups of people within many churches, and would be administered at the same time. The two assessments developed for group use were to be administered twice, one year apart. Conclusions concerning spiritual growth were extracted from the assessments by comparing the answers from the two assessments. Two assessments administered one year apart will result in two snapshots of the spiritual condition of those completing the assessment.

Several things can influence the responses to the questions: a person's health, emotional experience the day of administration, family issues, financial issues, answering questions the way the individual thinks the administrator wants them to answer. Definitive conclusions might be problematic.

Conclusions taken from the research:

- A Measuring Spiritual Maturity program should be developed for the church. Each participant is to have a level of responsibility for spiritual growth. However, the church has a responsibility to assist the members, and others, in growing spiritually.
- The Measuring Spiritual Maturity program should be part of a disciple-making process to be developed by the church.
- A participating church should be given the opportunity to customize the Measuring Spiritual Maturity program.
- A Measuring Spiritual Maturity organizational structure is to be presented in the material. The organizational structure should be *church-size* and *volunteer-time* sensitive.
- The assessment should be administered multiple times to each participant. Multiple administrations will allow participants to visualize their progress toward spiritual maturity. Multiple administrations will allow participants to complete the assessment based on their own thoughts rather than responding to outside elements.
- The assessment questions should include more than the usual questions shown on the fourteen spiritual-growth surveys examined during the research. It has been sug-

gested a section relating to the Fruit of the Spirit be added to the assessment.

- Confidentiality should be a high priority in the Measuring Spiritual Maturity program.
- Cornerstone Consultants LLC could provide consultation services as requested by the church. Consultation fees are to be church-financial and church-size sensitive.

# CHAPTER 2

## Introduction

*MEASURING SPIRITUAL MATURITY IS A PROCESS
TO BE USED TO INDICATE THE PROGRESS OF
INDIVIDUALS TOWARD SPIRITUAL MATURITY.*

*A* major responsibility of the church is to reach people who are outside the family of God and, more importantly, assist people who are inside the family of God to experience spiritual growth. The basis for this statement is found in one Scripture: "[18]All authority in heaven and on earth has been given to me. [19] Therefore go and make disciples of all nations, baptizing them in the name of the Father and of the Son and of the Holy Spirit, [20] and teaching them to obey everything I have commanded you."[1] The command is clearly stated to "make disciples." Within that directive there are two actions: "baptism" and "teaching."

As we begin exploring Measuring Spiritual Maturity, we will examine what some may misconstrue as the reason for the development of this disciple-making program. Measuring Spiritual Maturity is not an attempt to supplant the importance of evangelism through the church. It is not meant to be a battle between evangelism and discipleship.

The foundation of Measuring Spiritual Maturity is designed to encourage church leaders to follow the commands given by Jesus

---

[1]   *The New International Version*. (2011). (Mt 28:18–20). Grand Rapids, MI: Zondervan.

in the Great Commission in the correct priority order. Measuring Spiritual Maturity is a unique study of the spiritual development of members of churches and religious groups. Make no mistake about it. Churches must pursue evangelism. What good does it do to bring new Christians into churches filled with people who are spiritually shallow? Therefore, discipleship and evangelism are very important. This idea will be developed further in chapter 3.

Measuring Spiritual Maturity is a unique process. The uniqueness of Measuring Spiritual Maturity is not necessarily in the survey portion of the process. Most assessments use the same, or close to the same, questions. The main differences in the assessments are in the administration of the assessment, the scoring of the assessment, and the follow-up to each administration of the assessment.

Twelve of the fourteen assessments studied in the research phase were self-administered. One of the assessments was administered by a company, and one assessment was to be administered by a friend selected by the individual taking the assessment. Twelve of the fourteen assessments were administered only one time. Two assessments were to be administered twice. The second administration of these two assessments was one year after the first administration. The developers of these two assessments claimed the difference between the two administrations would give an indication of the spiritual growth/decline of the person who completed the assessments.

Thirteen of the fourteen assessments were scored by the individual who completed the assessment, or a friend selected by the individual. One assessment was scored by the company that provided the assessment. The assessment developed by a consulting company was the only assessment with a follow-up plan. A representative of the company would consult with the individual who completed the assessment or consult with a representative of the church.

The administration of the Measuring Spiritual Maturity assessment is also different from other spiritual growth surveys in several ways. First, the flexibility of administration is based on church size, structure, etc. Secondly, multiple administrations of the survey should span a stated amount of time, which gives an opportunity to create a visual that will indicate the progress of the individual taking the survey. A process that has one administration of a survey will only be able to obtain a glimpse of what the individual completing the survey is thinking, feeling, or experiencing at the time the survey is completed.

A survey with two administrations several months apart will provide insight for the time frame of each administration, but will not allow the person interpreting the results of the survey to develop conclusions by connecting the two administrations. However, when a survey is administered four or five times during a one-month, three-month, six-month, nine-month, or twelve-month time frame, the confidence level of the results of the assessment will significantly increase. Thirdly, a support system that is church developed and church staffed will assist those participating in the process. The fourth uniqueness is a measurement tool used to allow the individual to self-evaluate with the assistance of an assigned mentor. As each administration is completed and the scores are entered into the measurement tool, a tracking line is created, giving a visual depiction of each element of the assessment. This visual presentation will provide the individuals a way to express their feelings and ideas concerning their spiritual growth. The mentor will add comments as needed.

The Measuring Spiritual Maturity process is designed to provide an organizational structure to assist the church staff in conducting the spiritual maturity assessment process. The organizational structure will also provide a method to add new individuals who wish to be a part of the assessment process. The organization structure is church-size sensitive and is flexible to fit into any church-ministry plan. The Measuring Spiritual Maturity organizational structure will provide a way to prevent work overload on church staff and lay leaders.

Several interesting, expected, and unexpected questions and responses emerged during the months of constructing the Measuring Spiritual Maturity process. People would constantly inquire about the title and content of the book. The response would simply be to state the title, "Measuring Spiritual Maturity." Every time the title was mentioned two things would happen. First, a statement would be, "You can't measure spiritual maturity!" and immediately, a question would follow: "Why would you want to measure something that cannot be measured?" While the statement is true, it is not accurate.

The statement that you cannot measure spiritual maturity is a true statement in the eyes of many church leaders because popular belief is that spiritual maturity is a spiritual experience with no physical actions. The statement that you cannot measure spiritual maturity is not accurate because writers in the New Testament paint a picture of levels of spiritual growth. Paul did not think spiritual growth was unrecognizable when he wrote to the church at Corinth in 1 Corinthians 3:1–3. He called those Christians "babies in Christ." He also stated he had given them spiritual milk rather than spiritual solid food because they were not ready for solid food.

Peter also did not think spiritual maturity was unimportant, as illustrated when he wrote in 1 Peter 2:2 they needed spiritual milk in order to grow into maturity. The writer of Hebrews also had the opinion spiritual maturity was a process and not an instant event: "Now everyone who lives on milk is inexperienced with the message about righteousness, because he is an infant. But solid food is for the mature—for those whose senses have been trained to distinguish between good and evil" (Hebrews 5:12–14, HCSB). The idea of measuring the progress toward spiritual maturity is valid because various levels of spiritual maturity exist.

The question of why anyone would want to measure the spiritual-maturity process is an easy question to answer. A connection between spiritual growth and becoming a disciple is apparent. Becoming a disciple is second in importance to spiritual growth. The reason for this juxtaposition can be understood by recognizing that an individual cannot become a disciple without growing spiritually. However, a person who is growing spiritually can become a disciple.

Robby Gallaty, Senior Pastor of Long Hollow Baptist Church in Hendersonville, Tennessee, clarified the connection between spiritual growth and discipleship in an interview given to a writer of *Facts & Trends* Magazine on February 20, 2018. Gallaty stated, "Believers who are discipled begin to grow exponentially. The pipeline for service and volunteerism in our church is disciple-making groups. The byproduct of spiritual maturity is numeric growth…Jesus never left disciple-making to chance. He was intentional with His twelve disciples from the outset of their calling."[2] Further discussion of the relationship between discipleship and spiritual growth will be presented in chapter 3.

There seems to be little agreement about the basics of discipleship. Even with the number of discussions, sermons, books, articles, etc., on the topic, no consistent, repeatable definition of discipleship, course of action for discipleship, or an indication of when a person achieves the level of being discipled can be found. We need to take a general look at the modern-day concept of discipleship before we study the elements of spiritual maturity. A suitable concept for discipleship for all churches will not happen with one book, one sermon, one conference, one school course, or one multimedia presentation.

The concept of discipleship should be determined by each church and/or spiritual group. The old saying certainly fits here: one size does not fit all situations. The discipleship format for a Methodist church may look entirely different from the discipleship format of a Baptist church. In fact, there may not be two Baptist or two Methodist churches with the same discipleship format. A Catholic Church will probably not use a discipleship format that resembles a Pentecostal Church's discipleship format. The same could be said for any church, denomination, or religious group. This diversity will likely remain until God unites all His children under one spiritual roof called heaven.

Some items need to be clarified by all churches, denominations, religious groups, or sects as the discipleship format is crafted:

1. An examination of how a disciple-making process fits into the life of the church, group, or sect
2. A workable definition of a disciple
3. Determining the prerequisites for being a disciple
4. Defined components of the disciple-making process

---

2  Robby Gallaty, Developing A Culture of Discipleship in Your Church, (Facts & Trends Magazine, Nashville: Lifeway Christian Resources, 2018).

5. An answer to the question of how the advancement from spiritual babyhood to spiritual adulthood will be measured
6. The end result of discipleship

The material in this book is designed to give church leaders information and ideas to develop a disciple-making process. The material is not designed to tell the church leader what must be done in the discipleship format of the church. That is not the prerogative of this writer. This material has not been put together as the one and only definitive information on Spiritual Maturity. Developing the discipleship format remains in the hands of pastors, church leaders, and church members. The material is also not designed to take the place of the discipleship format currently in the church. This material is designed to give food for thought and items to add or to reconfigure the current discipleship format.

An extensive bibliography is provided at the conclusion of this material. The list of resources is to give direction in finding other views concerning discipleship.

# CHAPTER 3

## *Discipleship for the Church*

*A* disciple-making process should not be an add-on feature to the menu of activities for the church. It is to be a process that is developed, promoted, adopted, and recognized by the members of the church. A disciple-making process is to be built on the bedrock of everything the church believes and does. Because all ministries in the church should be born from the disciple-making process, a written disciple-making guide should be created to move individuals from a position of little or no spiritual knowledge toward a position of spiritual maturity.

One undeniable fact about spiritual maturity is that it will be completed only as a person passes through the gates of heaven. Even though that fact is true, the journey toward spiritual maturity is to be started and continued in this lifetime. Most church leaders have had the experience of knowing a person who seemed to be a little closer to God than everyone else.

Recall an individual or individuals whom the church members call "saints." When the church listens to a "saint" pray out loud, there is a feeling of being in the throne room of God. When a "saint" is encountered in life situations, they have a peace surrounding their countenance. They are pleasant to be around and enjoy talking about spiritual matters as well as things of this world. None of these attributes happened accidentally or overnight. "Saints" have had a long experience of spiritual growth. They are the people who are to be held in high esteem and emulated.

The disciple-making process should not be written or constructed in the format of an organizational constitution or a set of corporation by-laws. These two types of documents are usually wordy and command language written in a legalistic style. Even though it is important that the church have all legal documents that are required, those legal documents can be changed without regard to spiritual matters. The disciple-making process should only be changed when a spiritual belief of the church changes and should be written in a style understood by the members of the church.

Books, leaflets, conferences, seminars, associations, conventions, colleges, or seminaries are good places to gain information and ideas about discipleship. However, these resources are not good for the detailed development of the disciple-making process for the church. They are good for giving general ideas and options for consideration for placement into a disciple-making process. Remember, the disciple-making process for the church is *for the church*. It may contain some elements from other places, but it should be unique to the church.

The wording of the written disciple-making process should be simple and easily understood. Ecclesiastical or legal language should be used sparingly in writing the disciple-making process. The wording of the document should be the language of the people in the church. The written disciple-making process should be revisited on a regular basis (i.e., once every several years). This review of the vernacular of the written process will insure the language of the document is compatible with the language of the current congregation.

Many hours of prayer, thought, and involvement of people in the church will be the building blocks for developing a disciple-making process for the church. Prayer is the primary element because God knows more about what the church needs than anybody else. Tap into that resource and let God guide you. Praying for wisdom in developing a disciple-making process must be more involved than a one-minute prayer that is uttered to open and close meetings.

The following example illustrates how prayer can guide the decision-making process. One church was making some decisions for the future. The pastor announced that sign-up sheets were available for one-hour time slots for prayer. This season of prayer was designed for forty days. Volunteers were to come to the church for their time of prayer. Prayer was offered each hour for twenty-four hours for forty days. A tremendous spiritual time came out of that experience. Prayer for the development of a disciple-making process must be intentional, purposeful, and meaningful.

The disciple-making process will need to have a training component. An essential part of training people is often missing from modern training exercises. In times past, "thinking it through" meant the planners were to consider all elements from the beginning to the end before launching the event or training people to lead the event. It was not necessarily a pattern of thought that was important, but it was the time and opportunity to calmly and quietly think.

In a culture of instant gratification, we want to skip quickly from the idea stage to the participation stage. Remember this verse: "Do not be shaped by this world; instead be changed within by a new way of thinking. Then you will be able to decide what God wants for you; you will know what is good and pleasing to him and what is perfect" (Romans 12:2, Everyday Bible: New Century Version). An old adage may be good for today's church leaders: "There is nothing wrong with sittin' and whittling before you get up to start doin' somethin'."

Church leaders return home from attending a conference, camp, meeting, or retreat ready to implement the latest and greatest thing they heard at the event. It is better for church leaders to think through several questions before plunging ahead. Consider a few questions that will allow you to have a time of thought: Is this idea a really good idea? Does this idea fit the beliefs of our church? Will this idea assist our church in fulfilling our goals? What can we do to adjust the idea so it will work for us?

Another action that will give time for thought is to visit a friend who is not a member of the church and discuss the idea with that person. This is not putting together a plan, but merely attempting to see the idea from another person's point of view and hear an outside opinion. I had just left a ministry leadership position, and a close friend had accepted the position. In the years that followed his acceptance, he would call to discuss an idea he would like to try. I came to understand that he already had thought about 90 percent of the thoughts I would share. However, it was the 10 percent he had not considered that made the visits valuable to him.

Involvement of additional people in planning a new program, ministry, or event is critical to the success of the planning process. Church leaders who feel they are called to the church to provide all the answers are deceiving themselves. God does not call people to churches to see everything, be everything, and know everything. The only "everything" God calls church leaders to be is "all in" to God. The church leader is to be the leader of the church with a supporting cast of planners.

A pastor of a single staff church could assemble a development group of church members who are seen as spiritually minded. This group may or may not be deacons, elders, or other elected officials. The pastor and the development group would be assigned to write the disciple-making process. A pastor of a multiple-staff church, even if it is just the pastor and one other, could have an additional step in the development process. The pastor and church staff would begin the process of developing the disciple-making process.

As development progresses past the basic elements of the process, additional team members, who are considered to be spiritually minded, could be added to the development group. Again, this group may or may not be deacons, elders, or other elected officials.

Measuring the progress toward spiritual maturity should be a high priority in the development in the disciple-making process. The measurement should be accomplished using a measurement tool. Many church leaders have the erroneous opinion that they can measure the spiritual maturity level of the membership by studying attendance in worship services and Bible study programs. If that is the case, the church in America is in sad shape. Church statistics shown in the 2010 US Religion Census for 235 religious denominations and religious groups indicate only 21% of the 150,686,156 members, children, and other attenders participated in worship services. An additional study of the 2017 statistics of one state in a Baptist denomination indicated only 30% of the 44,913 church members attended worship and 19% of the church members attended the ongoing Bible study program. American churches seem to be doing a poor job of disciple-making if attendance in worship services and Bible study groups are the only indicators being monitored.

Measuring Spiritual Maturity was created to give church leaders a visual to gauge what is taking place in the spiritual lives of the members of their church. In order to obtain this information, the spiritual maturity assessment needs to be administered several times over a desired period of time. If you want to gain vital information, you must put some effort into the process. That truth applies to almost anything in life. We cannot expect a football team to practice one day a week and be proficient in winning games. We cannot expect an accountant to read one book and become an expert in advising us about our taxes. The same metaphors can be used for doctors, teachers, lawyers, or scientists. Spiritual growth should command the same attention and preparation as other elements of society. The details concerning the administration of the assessment are provided for you in chapter 7.

The written disciple-making process need not be a long document. In fact, research for this book revealed that Jesus only had four steps in his disciple-making process: Follow, Learn, Believe, and Act. The programming put into place by the church to accomplish the disciple-making process may be much more detailed.

If you search the Gospels and list all the actions and activities you find that fall under each of the four areas of Jesus's disciple-making process, you will have many pages of material to use as examples. The Follow, Learn, Believe, and Act strategy will be explored in chapter 4; however, people who search the Scriptures may identify other multistep discipling processes in the four Gospels. People interpret Scripture in different ways. Find the outline that best serves your needs.

Keep in mind two important things as the Gospels are searched for an outline of Jesus's disciple-making process. First, it will be a multistep process. Guiding an individual from a person who does not believe Christ is the Son of God to a person growing toward being a maturing Christian cannot be accomplished in one step. Second, as each step of a disciple-making process is discovered, the "Why" question must be addressed. For example, the most used definition of a disciple is "a person who is a follower." Why questions may be, "Why is the person asked to follow someone? Why is the follower to do as they are instructed?" The person identifying the disciple-making process should be able to explain in detail "why" each step is important to the process. Jesus invested Himself in discipling the twelve men who were with Him for several years for a specific purpose. The "why" is almost as important as the "what."

The final step in the development of a disciple-making process is the creation of a plan to execute the disciple-making process. The tendency of church leaders is to do things quickly rather than patiently. After hearing a detailed presentation about Measuring Spiritual Maturity, one pastor proclaimed he could use the results of the assessment to help him plan sermons. He concluded his remarks by saying, "I am going to administer this to the entire congregation!"

It is better to start with a small administration of the assessment and grow from that experience. Accepting the realization of spiritual growth of members of the church is not a hundred-yard dash. It is closer to a marathon and will allow you to evaluate more results. The more information gathered over a period of time, the better the insight will be for follow-up activities and events.

Measuring Spiritual Maturity is a product that can be used with individuals or any size group. The author recommends the first use of the assessment is more productive with individuals, such as church staff, Bible study leaders, deacons, or elders. After a cycle of administrations of the assessment has been completed, the disciple-making process planning group can decide to whom the next cycle of administrations will be given.

Two issues about spiritual growth assessment administration are very important. First, if the administration of the assessment is to an identified group of people (i.e., a Bible study class or group), not everyone in the class or group will accept the invitation to participate. That response is fine. It is better to administer the assessment to one half of the class rather than not conduct the administration because one half of the class rejected the invitation. More information will be given about this situation further into this material.

Second, it is important to remember that in order to create a visual representing the progress toward spiritual maturity, the assessment will need to be administered multiple times to the same individuals. One or two administrations of the assessment will only give you a limited snapshot of the progress of individuals who completed the assessment.

# CHAPTER 4

## A Definition of a Disciple

*B*ill Hull stated church leaders have used the word *disciple* with no clear definition.[3] This lack of a clear definition of a disciple creates confusion. Some of the definitions of a disciple are: "All true believers were disciples" (Gordon Smith)[4]; "A disciple is someone who seeks spiritual growth, possesses vital faith, lives a Christian life, practices your faith, has a positive spirit, be of service, and exhibits moral responsibility" (Oswald Sanders)[5]; "A disciple as a follower" (George Gallup)[6].

In addition to the confusion created by several definitions is the use of various titles for discipleship. Waggoner wrote that New Testament discipleship had at least three elements: becoming a disciple, living as a disciple, and growing as a disciple.[7] Some writers have used the individual elements of discipleship to mean the total process of discipleship. Gordon Smith used the term "spiritual formation" as the concept of discipleship.[8] Thomas Bergler used the term

---

[3] Bill Hull, *The Disciple-making Pastor*, Kindle 72.

[4] Gordon Smith, *Called to Be Saints: An Invitation to Christian Maturity*, Kindle 2148.

[5] J. Oswald Sanders, *Spiritual Maturity: Principles of Spiritual Growth for Every Believer (Commitment to Spiritual Growth)*, Kindle 3158–3207.

[6] George Gallup in: Randy Frazee, The Christian Life Profile (Grand Rapids, MI: Zondervan, 2005). 1.

[7] Brad Waggoner, *The Shape of Faith to Come*, Kindle 298.

[8] Gordon Smith, *Called to Be Saints,* Kindle 60.

"spiritual maturity" as the concept of discipleship.[9] Sanders used the terms "spiritual maturity" and "spiritual growth" as the concept of discipleship.[10]

With the multitude of titles for discipleship, it appears a comprehensive discipleship plan would need to include a spiritual formation element to begin the disciple-making process, a spiritual growth element to explore how to live as a Christian, a spiritual maturity element to chart progress toward Christian living, and a spiritual accountability element to ensure the correct path is being followed. Imagine how long a document would have be to chronicle the definition and examples of these four elements.

Those who have reduced their thoughts concerning disciples to written materials have added to the confusion. Thomas Bergler stated that *discipleship* is one of the words used to describe different perspectives on spiritual growth.[11] Bergler also wrote that when Christ called His disciples, He also called them to spiritual transformation.[12] Brad Waggoner attributed disciples as being "all true believers."[13] J. Oswald Sanders wrote the Lord "demands unconditional discipleship."[14] Gordon Smith identifies "a Christian is to be a disciple of Jesus," but then expands the term to include "mature disciple".[15] Bill Hull expressed his idea concerning a definition of a disciple by writing, "The definition has proven elusive. Is a disciple a convert, one who has simply trusted in Christ alone for his salvation?

[9] Thomas Bergler, *From Here to Maturity: Overcoming the Juvenilization of American Christianity.* Kindle 4259.

[10] Sanders, *Spiritual Maturity,* Kindle 24.

[11] Thomas Bergler, *From Here to Maturity: Overcoming the Juvenilization of American Christianity* (Grand Rapids, MI: William B Eerdmans, 2014), Kindle 1350.

[12] Ibid, Kindle 724.

[13] Waggoner, *The Shape of Faith to Come* (Nashville, TN: Scott, 2008), Kindle 168.

[14] Sanders, *Spiritual Maturity: Principles of Spiritual Growth for Every Believer (commitment to Spiritual Growth)* (Chicago, IL: Moody Bible Institute, 1994), Kindle 925.

[15] Gordon Smith, *Called to Be Saints: An Invitation to Christian Maturity* (Downers Grove, IL: InterVarsity Press, 2014), Kindle 511.

Is it more, a fruit-bearing, reproducing believer described by Jesus in other passages? Or it is only for the totally committed person whom Jesus described in Luke 14:25–35, who puts Christ before possessions, self, and family?"[16]

Michael Kelly, speaking at the 2017 annual meeting of the Baptist Association of Christian Educators, stated that we tend to over complicate what discipleship is: "We trick ourselves into thinking we are doing something when in actuality we are just talking about it."[17] Church leaders think the disciple-making process is actually producing disciples when worship and Bible study attendance has increased and/or baptisms have increased. Robby Gallaty stated in an interview with a Facts and Trends writer in 2018, "In a church where disciple-making focuses solely upon the decisions, the process of walking with new converts is often minimized or set at such a low priority people simply don't understand the importance."[18]

The first step in defining a disciple for the church is to recognize discipleship is not a project but a process. Becoming a disciple is not a short, one-step action and cannot be defined with one word. The definition for a disciple should be a short phrase, and each church leader should develop the phrase for his or her ministry. One such phrase is "Growing from an awareness of God toward spiritual maturity by following the outline Jesus used." Jesus's use of a well-defined outline is not readily apparent until you begin to study how Jesus worked with the men He chose as apostles. Jesus used four steps as His disciple-making process. These four steps are not found in one location in the New Testament but throughout the Gospels.

[16] Bill Hull, *The Disciple-making Pastor: Leading Others on the Journey of Faith* (Grand Rapids, MI: Baker Books, 2007), Kindle 930.
[17] Michael Kelley, Director of Discipleship, LifeWay Christian Resources, speaking at the BACE annual meeting April 2017 at New Orleans Baptist Theological Seminary.
[18] Robby Gallaty, Developing A Culture of Discipleship in Your Church, (Facts & Trends Magazine, Nashville: Lifeway Christian Resources, 2018).

## Step 1: Follow

The command to follow Jesus has become the most important element of the disciple-making process to many church leaders. More often than not, it is stated as the only step in guiding an
individual toward spiritual maturity. Several pastors engaged in discussions concerning discipleship during a two-year time frame of
research by the author of this book. The direction of the conversations led the author to ask why a person is to follow Jesus. A majority
of the pastors responded, "To be like Jesus." That response led to a
second question: "In what way are we to be like Jesus?" Usually the
response to the second question was either "To be close to God" or
"To be concerned about and caring for other people." While it is true
that Christians are to emulate Jesus's life on earth, the open-ended
response "To be like Jesus" gives no specific direction. Following
Jesus may simply mean wanting to know more about the man identified as the Son of God. Following Jesus may mean an individual
becomes aware of a spiritual life that God is offering. Pastors should
lead their congregations to decide and adopt a clearly stated definition of following Jesus.

The idea that a disciple is an individual that follows a leader is
not a new concept. It has been in practice throughout Old Testament
times. Most people define a disciple as a follower because Jesus asked
His disciples to follow Him (Matthew 4:18–22; Mark 1:16, 3:17).
The instruction to follow Jesus is not debatable. It is plainly stated in
Scripture. In fact, the statement to follow Jesus may not have been
an invitation but a command. Ronald Kernaghan stated in his commentary on the Gospel of Mark the statement to follow was a direct
command.[19] The idea of issuing a direct command may not be such a
far-fetched idea when the prior relationship between Andrew, Simon,
James, John, and Jesus is examined.

Andrew was an ardent follower of John the Baptizer (John
1:40–42). When Andrew heard John the Baptizer announce Jesus

---

[19] Ronald J. Kernaghan, *The IVP New Testament Commentary Series: Mark*
(Downers Grove, Il: InterVarsity Press, 2007), 44.

as the Messiah, Andrew brought Simon to Jesus. Andrew and Simon were in a fishing business together with James and John. It was a natural progression for Andrew to bring the other three to meet Jesus. The four men were working for their fathers who were partners in the fishing business. The friendship between these four fishermen and Jesus took place at least a year before the command to follow was issued. During that year, the four men would occasionally leave their fishing jobs and spend short periods of time with Jesus and return to their vocations.

The answer to why would Jesus issue such a command can be found in two important facts. First, when Jesus saw Andrew and Simon, as recorded in Matthew and Mark, He did not see two men He did not know. He saw two men that needed to move from being bi-vocational followers to being full-time followers. The command to follow was a command to change vocations. The same was true with the command given to James and John just down the shoreline. It is possible during the previous year the relationship between these five men was an off-again and on-again situation. At various times, one or more of these four fishermen would travel to see Jesus, stay with Him for a short time, and return to their business. Jesus wanted to train them for a different type of work, and their respect for Jesus allowed Jesus to issue a command to follow Him. Why else would four men leave a family business and strike out with a stranger?

Second, it would be appropriate for Jesus to have explained the reason for asking them to follow Him if it had been a simple invitation, He would have explained what He was asking them to do. However, no record of Jesus explaining what He was expecting them to do exists. They were not being enlisted, at this point, to preach, heal, cast out evil spirits, or debate. They were to observe. Jesus wanted them to see how God was going to work through humans in a different way. If they simply watched Jesus at work doing God's business, they would be ready to do God's business themselves when it was time for Jesus to leave.

Not all of the apostles were asked to follow Jesus. We have a record of Andrew, Simon, James, John, Philip (John 1:43), and Matthew (Mark 2:14). We do not have a record of six of the apostles being asked or commanded to follow. The "Follow me" statement may have simply been omitted by the authors of the Gospels. However, this reason does not seem valid since "Follow me" was included by the same author that omitted that phrase for the other six apostles. Another reason may be the six that did not receive the "Follow me" command were not approached by Jesus but brought to Jesus by someone already in the group. We know Philip and Mathew were introduced to Jesus by Andrew. The only conclusion that can be drawn from this observation is being a follower by itself will not make a person a disciple.

## Step 2: Learn

Another one-word definition for a disciple is *learner*. The idea assumes that a disciple will attach himself to a teacher and soak in all the information dispensed by the teacher. This concept is good but limited because a disciple is more than just a learner.

Life is a journey of learning. From the day we were born until the day we die, we are constantly learning. Consistent learning is not only a general concept but also a specific concept in all areas of life. We learned to eat, walk, play, and interact with others as we progressed from preschoolers to children. As children we learned new ideas and concepts as we began and worked our way through "formal education." In the youth segment of life, we began the process of learning how to apply those ideas, concepts, and information into real-life situations. We also began to learn about relationships. In the adult area of life, we began to realize the world doesn't always stay the same. It is constantly changing, and we have to learn to keep current of the changes without compromising our beliefs.

Disciple-making (spiritual maturity) requires a similar intensive learning process. Jesus recognized this pattern and interjected learning opportunities into the lives of the apostles through the observation process and direct instruction. An example of learning from observation is recorded in Mark 11:13–14, 20–21 when Jesus cursed the fig tree, and the next day the apostles saw the tree was withered.

Another example is found in Mark 12:41–44 when Jesus taught the apostles about the gift of the widow.

An example of direct instruction is found in Matthew 5–7. The assumption concerning this passage has been that Jesus was delivering a sermon to the large crowd that had gathered on the hillside. An important phrase is at the beginning of the story of the Sermon on the Mount in Matthew 5:1: "…after He sat down." The action Jesus took of sitting was not unusual at that period of time. Rabbis would sit to teach in the synagogues. The Scripture also states, "His disciples came to Him."

It is unfortunate the word *disciple* is used in the Gospels as a reference for both the apostles and the crowds of people. R. T. France wrote the crowd of people was a remote audience and the main audience was the Twelve.[20] The concept of the Twelve as the main focus of Jesus's presentation is verified by W. H. Mare when he wrote, "The text says that He began to teach His disciples who had come to Him indicating that Jesus' sermon was primarily addressed to His professed disciples, with the crowds listening in."[21]

The question of whom Jesus taught and who were just listeners becomes important because it changes how we view the Sermon on the Mount. If the crowd was the focal point of the lecture, the purpose of the content would have been telling them how they were to live. If the Twelve were the focal point of Jesus's presentation, He was delivering the concepts the Twelve were to live *and* what they were to teach to others. Craig Keener has pointed out Matthew had summarized Jesus's message earlier in the book. Jesus now explains a guide to living for the repentant person.[22]

Jesus may not have been presenting a sermon but teaching a lesson. He may have been giving the apostles the concepts and ideals He wanted them to learn and teach to those they discipled. The

---

[20] France, R. T. (1985). *Matthew: an introduction and commentary* (Vol. 1, p. 113). Downers Grove, IL: InterVarsity Press.

[21] Mare, W. H. (2004). *New Testament Background Commentary: A New Dictionary of Words, Phrases and Situations in Bible Order* (p. 21). Ross-shire, UK: Mentor.

[22] Keener, C. S. (1997). *Matthew* (Vol. 1, Mt 5:1). Downers Grove, IL: InterVarsity Press.

crowd happened to be in a place that was a natural amphitheater that allowed them to hear the instruction being given to the apostles. It would become vital for the apostles to know and accept these concepts as they began spreading the Gospel and establishing churches. The building blocks for living life as a Christian and experiencing spiritual growth are found in Matthew 5–7. The process for gaining entrance into the Christian life will be given later.

## Step 3: Believe

In today's evangelism culture, the condition of belief is at the forefront of the spiritual journey an individual is asked to pursue. It is interesting to note Jesus did not bring up the question of the apostles believing Him to be the Messiah until after they had been together as a unit for some time. It may be argued Jesus wanted to see some spiritual growth in the Twelve before He approached the question that would cause them to vocally state their belief. R. T. France wrote "the response to Jesus' question was the climax of the gradual recognition of the Messiah by his disciples during the Galilean period."[23]

A friend once stated that salvation is not reciting a formula or following some outline. The point of salvation happens when there is an *encounter with God*. Some people have that encounter with God at the beginning of their disciple-making process. Other people begin their spiritual growth process before experiencing that encounter with God. Therefore, the belief in and acceptance of Jesus as Savior are very much a part of the spiritual growth process, but are not locked down at a specific point in the spiritual journey.

The placement of the question "Who do people say that the Son of Man is?" in Mark 8 is unusual because it is just thrust out with no preamble or lead-in. It is as if the twelve men had huddled around Jesus for the entire journey and then suddenly Jesus asks the

---

[23] France, R. T. (2007). *The Gospel of Matthew* (p. 612). Grand Rapids, MI: Wm. B. Eerdmans Publication Co.

question. Paul Harvey's famous commentary line works very well at this point: "And now the rest of the story."

The journey that took Jesus and the apostles to the area of Caesarea Philippi was not an easy or short stroll. It was a 25-mile trek up 1,700 feet in altitude. Commentators speculate it took three days to make the journey. Jesus very seldom was able to travel anywhere without a crowd of people joining Him, and such was the case on this trip. The apostles would not have traveled the entire 25 miles huddled around Jesus. Several times the apostles, either individually or as a group, intermingled with the crowd. Given these conditions, a reason for Jesus to open the line of questions to His men emerges. The first question was not the primary reason for the interrogation. Jesus wanted to hear where they were spiritually and to see if Simon would step forward and finally become the leader of the group.[24] Belief was not a prerequisite for the journey but a by-product of personal experiences and relational growth.

## Step 4: Act

Spiritual growth would be only an educational experience without an action, or actions, to demonstrate the movement of an individual from a spiritual baby toward a maturing Christian. The action process, as stated in the Great Commission (Matthew 28:18–20), is the final step in the disciple-making process. However, in today's religious culture, too many church leaders have diluted the Great Commission into an evangelism directive. The Great Commission is not an evangelism directive, a teaching directive, or a going directive. The Great Commission is a multi-faceted disciple-making directive.

H. M. Haller wrote, "Contrary to popular thought, the Great Commission in Matthew focuses on discipleship, not evangelism. Of course, to make disciples the Eleven had to evangelize so they would

---

[24] France, R. T. (2007). *The Gospel of Matthew* (p. 613). Grand Rapids, MI: Wm. B. Eerdmans Publication Co.

have believers to disciple."[25] Haller also stated the imperative in the verses of the Great Commission is *make disciples*: "The calls *to go, baptize,* and *teach* are all participles which are related to the action of the main verb."[26]

*Evangelism* is a part of the disciple-making process, but only one part. Some people label me as anti-evangelism. Nothing could be further from the truth. This material is about giving you an opportunity to view the Great Commission in a new light. Those who think evangelism is the most important element of a disciple-making process have the cart before the horse. Jesus has given us a plan that, if followed, will produce more evangelistic conversations and more baptisms than we are experiencing today. Many life metaphors can be used to show God's plan for growth. Metaphors that apply include these: a person must learn to crawl before learning to run, a boy does not go from sandlot baseball to a major league baseball team overnight, or a janitor does not become CEO of an existing company overnight.

Some churches that solely focus on evangelism have church activities in order to evangelize. Bible-study leaders are taught to expand their classes in order to evangelize. Courses instruct members how to formally and informally evangelize. Remember the command of the Great Commission is more than evangelism. The command is to *make disciples*. However, a good disciple-making process has an evangelism component. "In a church where disciple-making focuses solely upon the decisions, the process of walking with new converts is often minimized or set at such a low priority people simply don't understand the importance."[27]

---

[25] Haller, H. M., Jr. (2010). The Gospel according to Matthew. In R. N. Wilkin (Ed.), *The Grace New Testament Commentary* (p. 137). Denton, TX: Grace Evangelical Society.

[26] Haller, H. M., Jr. (2010). The Gospel according to Matthew. In R. N. Wilkin (Ed.), *The Grace New Testament Commentary* (p. 137). Denton, TX: Grace Evangelical Society.

[27] Robby Gallaty, Developing A Culture of Discipleship in Your Church, (Facts & Trends Magazine, Nashville: Lifeway Christian Resources, 2018).

Church leaders who consider a disciple-making process as the top priority of the Great Commission may come face to face with some interesting questions. One of those questions might be, "Does a person become a disciple without being a believer?" In seeking answers to these difficult questions in the four Gospel books, it might be interesting to ask, when did the Twelve become believers and when did they become disciples?

*Going* is a part of disciple-making and not the main function or the only function of disciple-making. Craig Bloomberg wrote, "Jesus' main focus remains on the task of all believers to duplicate themselves wherever they may be."[28]

Disciple-making must be a multifaceted process with all the parts being equal. An important aspect of disciple-making for the church is seeing individuals growing and maturing in Christ. Dr. David Brooks, Pastor of Calvary Baptist Church in Alexandria, Louisiana, stated in a sermon, "Invest your time in the undeveloped potential of others." The undeveloped potential of others is broader than one issue. It requires discovering the spiritual, mental, and life details of the one to be discipled. It also requires those who will be the disciplers to be trained in the fine points of disciple-making. It also requires disciple makers to be trained in leadership skills. An NFL analysist once commented leadership is not getting people to fall in behind you; it is getting them to join you.

When disciple-making is conducted as outlined in the Great Commission, the church will see increases in evangelism, baptisms, and membership. Most importantly, the church will function as an organized group with a central focus.

*Baptizing* is a part of the disciple-making process and not the main function or the only function of disciple-making. Baptism as a sign of repentance was brought to light by John the Baptizer:[11] "I baptize you with water for repentance. But after me comes one who is more powerful than I, whose sandals I am not worthy to carry. He

[28] Blomberg, C. (1992). *Matthew* (Vol. 22, p. 431). Nashville: Broadman & Holman Publishers.

will baptize you with the Holy Spirit and fire." [29] John's baptism was the first baptism of repentance in preparation for the coming of a specific Messiah.

Baptism had been a practice of the Jewish culture for many centuries. Their baptism was for purification, and public baptism areas had been established. The Essenes were Jewish individuals who had grown tired of the corruption within the temple leadership. The Essenes moved to the area next to the Dead Sea known as Quorum. In the twentieth century, the Dead Sea Scrolls were found in the Dead Sea area near where Quorum had been located. The Essenes continued baptism by immersion for repentance.

However, the repentance of the Essenes was the visible act of rejection of the corruption in Jerusalem. John joined the Essenes group, most likely as a child, and learned their ways. When John stepped forth to proclaim the coming of the Messiah, he brought with him the concept of baptism for repentance as preparation for the arrival of Jesus.

Jesus's baptism signaled a change in the purpose of baptism. Matthew 3 presents the account of Jesus's baptism: "[13]Then Jesus came from Galilee to John at the Jordan, to be baptized by him. [14] But John tried to stop Him, saying, 'I need to be baptized by You, and yet You come to me?' [15] Jesus answered him, 'Allow it for now, because this is the way for us to fulfill all righteousness.' Then he allowed Him to be baptized" (Matthew 3:13–15, HCSB).

The form of baptism that was used by John prior to Jesus's baptism did not change. The reason for the baptism did change. The voice from heaven announced and confirmed Jesus was the Son of God. Following Jesus's baptism, the purpose shifted to being a visual depiction of the spiritual change in the life of the one being baptized.

*Teaching* is a part of the disciple-making process and not the main function or the only function of disciple-making. Jesus used several different teaching styles in the discipling of the Twelve. Jesus used observation, conversation, discussion, and directives so the

---

[29] *The New International Version*. (2011). (Mt 3:11). Grand Rapids, MI: Zondervan.

Twelve could grasp what He was going to ask them to do. Many books are dedicated to the presentation and understanding of the teaching process. Those works will provide guidance in the teaching process. This section gives the reader information to ponder the purpose of teaching.

In its purest form, teaching is about presenting a concept, idea, belief, or plan to an individual or a group of individuals and then allowing the student(s) to work with what has been presented so the material becomes a part of their life and belief system. Teaching should not be just the dispensing of facts. An old saying that illustrates this concept: "Teaching facts is like packing meat into casings and making sausage. It may taste good while being consumed, but later you are not sure what you have eaten." Cramming pieces of meat into a sausage casing might produce a good meal, but cramming facts into the minds of students is not a good recipe for teaching, especially teaching the Bible. Students need to learn facts, but teaching involves much more than just the facts. Another old saying puts it this way: "Education is what is left after you have forgotten what you learned in school."

This is especially true for teachers of the Bible. It is important for the students to have the truths contained in the Bible presented to them. But that is only half of the teaching equation. The other half of Bible teaching is allowing the students to examine the biblical truth that is presented by the teacher and coming to an understanding of how that truth applies to their life. Teachers would do well to remember teaching is not about the teacher but about the student. A book written in the 1700s stated it this way: "The teacher teaches best who teaches least."[30]

---

[30] The Handbook of Sloyd by Otto Soloman.

# CHAPTER 5

## A Disciple-Making Process and Organization

*T*he process for making disciples is not, or should not, be a one-step process. As the disciple-making process is being established and maintained, please feel free to alter the contents of this chapter to fit the church size and philosophy. However a word of caution concerning customizing the organization of a disciple-making process is necessary: before any of the items are changed or deleted, ask the following question: "Will this change negatively impact the process?" Making a change because of size and/or philosophy may not negatively impact the process. Adjustments to the assessment and to the tally sheet can be done upon request. Simply removing a step because you do not want to do it may cause the results not to fulfill your desires. Make sure changes are made for sound, valid, and well-considered reasons.

### Define Disciple

The first step in the formation of a disciple-making process is to create a clear definition of a disciple. The definition of a disciple for the church should reflect the biblical and doctrinal position of the church. A person seeing or hearing the definition for the first time should be able to clearly understand what is being stated. Some definitions presented in chapter 4:

- a Christian is a disciple

- a disciple is a follower
- a disciple is a true believer
- anyone who has trusted Christ alone is a disciple
- a disciple is a fruit-bearing, reproducing believer

Each of these definitions are limited in helping an individual understand the meaning of being a disciple. Most of the definitions focus only on one aspect of a disciple. The definition of a disciple for the church should identify the various elements of being a disciple. Those elements include exhibiting the elements of the Fruit of the Spirit; studying of God's Word; communicating with God through prayer; participating in the community of church; engaging in the stewardship of time, talent, and finances; sharing faith; and recognizing of God, Jesus, baptism, worship, and service. A description of each of these elements should be consistent with the doctrinal belief and practical action of the church.

## Embrace a Willingness to Work

I have had the opportunity of working with over three thousand churches in the thirty-plus years I have been a consultant. Some church leaders understand the concept of process development. These leaders evaluate their strengths and weaknesses and begin to investigate how to improve their strengths and how to strengthen their weaknesses.

A majority of church leaders with whom Cornerstone Consultants, LLC has consulted are not willing to spend time evaluating and examining the ministries, programs, events, and processes currently within their church. They see a new program, ministry, or event being conducted by another church or recommended by a church leader and become excited to add it to the laundry list of their own church ministries or programs.

When church leaders or the church membership consider adding a new ministry or program, it takes time. It does not necessarily have to take years to implement something new. It could take a few weeks or a few months to conduct the reviews, enlist the leadership, provide training, and start the new ministry or program. Sadly, the world's concept of instant gratification has worked its way into the planning process of many church leaders.

The church staff and lay leaders will need to recognize and accept a time line of several months to develop, refine, staff, implement, and evaluate a disciple-making process. Starting with the pastor, the church staff, and lay leaders, a firm commitment will need to be established to evaluate the disciple-making process, develop the disciple-making process, enlist the correct people to lead the disciple-making process, fully explain to the church membership the goals of the disciple-making process, conduct the disciple-making process, and evaluate the results of the disciple-making process at the conclusion of each cycle.

## Establish a Disciple-Making Organization

The recommended size of the disciple-making organization and the number of people involved in the organization at first may seem overwhelming. The reader should keep in mind the following information is merely a suggestion. The size of the organization and the number of people enlisted to be involved in the disciple-making process will vary from church to church. The determining factor for the number of people to enlist as leaders in the disciple-making organization will be the size of the church membership and the number of people on the ministerial staff. A word of caution is valuable at this point. Do not have a church staff member or church member serve in more than one position within the disciple-making organization unless it is absolutely necessary.

- Pastor
    > The pastor is the spiritual leader of the church and therefore is the overseer of the disciple-making process.
    > The church may assign a committee to put together the disciple-making process, but it should be the pastor who ultimately oversees the work of the disciple-making team.

It is important for the pastor to receive general and summary reports of the progress of the disciple-making process.
› Confidentiality is a very important commodity in the disciple-making process except in extreme and critical situations.
› The pastor and staff may wish to give the disciple-making process a unique name.

- Administrator
  › The administrator is to oversee the disciple-making process.
  › The administrator may serve in more than one position if the number of students participating in the disciple-making process is ten or less.
  › The administrator is to be enlisted either by the pastor or a committee. If a committee is to enlist the administrator, the membership of the committee is to be determined by the church and include the pastor.
  › The administrator is to enlist, train, and monitor each person in the disciple-making organization: input person, Bible study group leader(s) (if the students will be enlisted from the members of the Bible study group or classes), and the mentors.
  › The administrator is to develop and lead the training meetings for the members of the disciple-making organization and to develop and lead an evaluation meeting at the conclusion of each cycle of the disciple-making process. A disciple-making cycle is defined as the time from the first administration of the assessment to the current students until the last administration of the assessment and a meeting of the mentors and students has taken place. A successive cycle may begin before the prior cycle has been completed. It is recommended that the disciple-making team determine the specified amount of time between a second cycle or third cycle of administration with the same students.

- Mentor
  - › The mentor in the disciple-making process is an important member of the disciple-making team.
  - › A mentor will guide individuals who participate in the disciple-making process through their spiritual growth experiences.
  - › It is recommended a mentor be enlisted for every three to five people who are taking the spiritual maturity assessment. The number of mentors to be enlisted will be determined by the number of people in the disciple-making process and the number of spiritual maturity assessment administrations given during a cycle. The number of mentors and the number of administrations will vary from church to church.
  - › A mentor in the disciple-making process is not necessarily someone who has all the answers.
  - › The main characteristic of a mentor is an individual who has a desire to see fellow church members grow in their spiritual life.
  - › Each disciple-making mentor will seek to extract an interpretation of the charts from the student, listen for information about the student's feelings, observe the student's emotional demeanor, and answer questions from the student, rather than prescribe what the individual needs to do. If the mentor interprets the data, provides details of information, recommends actions, answers questions before the question is asked, or declares solutions for emotions, the students will not learn how to discover these things.
  - › The information shared by the mentor to the individual should be very limited.
  - › A second characteristic of a mentor in the disciple-making process is patience. Patience requires the ability to listen with a clear mind and to formulate questions quickly. Listening is highly important for the mentor. It is not uncommon for a listener to begin to formulate a response before the student has completed a thought or question.

Being patient to hear the complete thought or question may influence the remarks and/or questions the mentor will give back to the student.

› Typically, the main response from the mentor to the student will be in the form of a question. This will allow the student to analyze what has been shared with the mentor and, hopefully, develop a conclusion or action.

› The mentor is to receive the charts for each assigned student within two weeks of each administration of the assessment.

› The mentor is to schedule a meeting with each assigned student within seven days of receiving the charts. The mentor is to give one set of charts to the student and retain a duplicate set of charts. It is suggested the mentor make notes on the mentor's copy of the charts. The charts are to be placed in a secured area in the church offices and can be retrieved prior to the next meeting.

› All information gleaned from the meetings between the mentor and the assigned students is confidential.

› The mentor may share a composite set of information with the pastor and/or the teacher/leader of a Bible study group where the student(s) is a member.

› Each mentor should be required to participate in a training event specifically designed for the mentors. The content of the training session is to provide information that will benefit the mentor in each session with each individual following each administration of the assessment. The information may include, but not be limited to, how to listen, how to formulate questions, how to observe body language, how to create a relaxed atmosphere during each meeting, and how and what to report to the administrator.

- Input person
  › The administrator is to enlist a person to enter the assessment information into an assessment tally sheet. The transfer of information is to be done at a computer so the charts can be generated.

> The input person is to produce copies of the assessment form to be given to the mentor to be given to the students to complete.

> The mentor will return the completed assessments to the input person who will enter the responses into the tally sheet.

> The input person will print two copies of all charts for each person who completed the assessment and give the charts to the mentor.

> The mentor will return one copy of the charts that contain notes made during the meeting with the student to the input person.

> The input person will place the mentor's charts and notes in a secure area following each administration of the assessment.

- Bible study group leader
  > If the church has an ongoing organized Bible study program, such as Sunday School or Life Groups, the leaders of each class or group should be provided a separate training event to inform them of the disciple-making process.

  > Bible study group leaders that have students participating in a disciple-making cycle may receive general updates from the mentors working with the students of their class or group. This information may be beneficial in the preparation of the lessons being presented in the class or group.

  > The mentors should not present any information identifying a specific student.

- Enlistment coordinator
  > The enlistment coordinator is assigned the responsibility of enlisting church members to participate in the disciple-making process.

  > General information concerning participation in the disciple-making process may be presented to various groups within the church. This could include during worship

services, Bible study groups, ministry group meetings, or fellowship groups. Part of the information shared in the group settings might include an invitation for those interested in participating in the process to visit with the enlistment coordinator or someone enlisted to assist the enlistment coordinator.

> It is recommended enlistment of individuals to participate in the disciple-making process be done in a one-on-one meeting.
> The confidential nature of the assessments and the meetings with a mentor should be a prominent part of the individual enlistment process.

- Training events
  > It is recommended three training events be conducted in connection with the disciple-making process.
  > The first training meeting will involve the pastor and each member of the church staff, and will be used to determine questions concerning the disciple-making process and to identify the person to be enlisted as the administrator. The administrator should be enlisted by the pastor and/or a committee be a part of all future meetings.
  > The remainder of the meetings of the planning group will focus on the details of the disciple-making process.
  > The second training meeting will be to train the members of the disciple-making leadership team: enlistment coordinator, input person, and mentors. The pastor should attend this training meeting to share his desire and importance of the disciple-making process. The administrator is to lead the remainder of the meeting. The content of the meeting is an overview of the process and a detailed description of each of the leadership team member's responsibilities.
  > The third training meeting will be led by the administrator. The church members who serve as teachers in teaching ministry groups—such as Bible study groups, missions study groups, special book study groups, etc.—are to attend this

meeting. Learning how members of the group are progressing toward spiritual maturity may impact a teacher's lesson preparation. The most important piece of information to be shared in this third training meeting is confidentiality. No teacher should receive assessment scores relating to one individual in the group. A summary of all the assessments scored should be prepared and given to the teacher during the disciple-making process following each administration of the assessment.

- A reporting system
    - > It is suggested a report be given to the church congregation at various times during a disciple-making process cycle. The frequency and detail of the reports is to be determined by the pastor, church staff, and the administrator.
    - > One suggestion is to present a general report at the beginning of a cycle, a second report close to halfway through the cycle, and a summary report at the conclusion of the cycle.
    - > It is important not to disclose any information that would single out an individual who is participating in the assessments.

# CHAPTER 6

## The Elements of the Measuring Spiritual Maturity Assessment

$A$ quality disciple-making process should be developed based on what Jesus considered important. The process should not be developed around the ideas of men. The foundation of building a disciple-making process is found throughout the Gospels. It is what Jesus spoke about and what the writers of the books of the New Testament explain.

The components of a disciple-making process are divided into two sections. The first section examines the characteristics of an individual who is striving to grow in their spiritual life. These characteristics are identified in Galatians 5:22–23. James Dunn has stated poignantly why Paul penned a list of the Fruit of the Spirit: "Paul's point then is that the nature of God's Spirit is demonstrated in the quality of character exemplified in the following list."[31] The elements of the Fruit of the Spirit are love, joy, peace, patience, kindness, goodness, faithfulness, gentleness, and self-control.

The second section outlines the activities of an individual who is engaged in a disciple-making process. The elements of actions in which a person in a disciple-making process should be engaged are prayer, Bible reading, community (church), stewardship, sharing faith, and foundations (which is comprised of and understanding of God, Jesus, the Bible, baptism, worship, and service).

---

[31] Dunn, J. D. G. (1993). *The Epistle to the Galatians* (p. 308). London: Continuum.

It will be beneficial for church leaders who are preparing a disci-ple-making process to define each of the elements in both sections of the assessment. The following information is meant to be a starting place for the development of the work of defining each element. The statistical data used to create the charts shown below is hypothetical and is presented for demonstration purposes.

Actual assessment data will generate charts similar to these charts. It is tempting for someone mentoring an individual who has taken the assessment to make determinations based on the peaks and valleys shown on each chart. The mentor is to guide the individual to express their feelings concerning the information contained on each chart. If the mentor senses a need to express some opinion, a summary statement could be made by the mentor of the entire chart.

## Love

Four Greek words, or some form of the words, can be translated as the word *love*, and three of these are used in the New Testament. The single Greek word that could be translated love but is not used in the New Testament is the word *eros*. *Eros* is used in the Greek language to communicate sexual love.[32] The word *phileo* is contained in the New Testament twenty-five times when the speaker is address-ing spontaneous natural affection and five times when addressing brotherly love—*philadelphia*. In one Scripture passage, the form of *phileo* refers to friendship. The Scripture is James 4:4, and the word is *philia*.

A third Greek word translated love is *storge*. *Storge* is used to discuss natural affection between kinfolk. Various forms of *agape* are used more than the other words that could be translated love. Generally, *agape* is used when the writer intends to convey the idea of moral goodwill between individuals or from an individual to a group of people. Examples of the use of *agape* can be found in Luke 11:42; John 5:42; Romans 5:8, 13:10; Galatians 5:13; Jude 1:21;

---

[32] White, R. E. O. (1988). Love. In *Baker encyclopedia of the Bible* (Vol. 2, p. 1357). Grand Rapids, MI: Baker Book House.

and Revelations 2:4. Love as part of the Fruit of the Spirit can be defined as "Love does no wrong to a neighbor. Love, therefore, is the fulfillment of the law" (Romans 13:10 Holman Christian Standard Bible).

The evaluation on the Spiritual Maturity Assessment about love is in question 1: "I rate the nine Fruit of the Spirit listed in Galatians 5:22–23 in my life as follows: (rate each fruit from 1–5: 1 = very weak; 5 = very strong)."

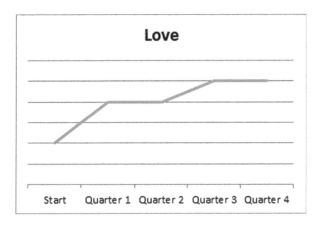

## Joy

Joy is a positive human condition that can be either state of being or feeling. Feeling is sometimes stated as an action. The Bible uses joy in both senses.[33] Joy can be an emotion and/or an action. When things in our life are going the way we think they should go and we are feeling happy, the emotion of joy colors our speech, determines our selection of words, and allows us to select various forms of movement to express our elated feeling.

Joy can also be an action, as seen in Matthew 8:8; Luke 2:10; Mark 11:9ff; Acts 13:52; 1 Peter 4:13; Galatians 5:22; James 1:2; Philippians 4:4; and 1 Thessalonians 5:16. Joy, as a Fruit of the Spirit

---

[33] Elwell, W. A., & Beitzel, B. J. (1988). Joy. In *Baker encyclopedia of the Bible* (Vol. 2, p. 1224). Grand Rapids, MI: Baker Book House.

relates to happiness, no matter what is happening around you. It is difficult to single out one scripture to represent this fruit. However, Acts 13:52 (NIV) is a good one to remember: "And the disciples were filled with joy and the Holy Spirit." James writes, "Consider it pure joy, my brothers and sisters, whenever you face trials of many kinds, knowing that the testing of your faith produces endurance" (James 1:2, HCSB).

How can trials and tribulations be confronted with pure joy? Dr. Waylon Bailey, Pastor First Baptist Church, Covington, Louisiana, wrote in his August 20, 2018, blog about this verse. Dr. Bailey states trials and tribulations can be pure joy; trials and tribulations can result in a closeness to God because to know that God cares for those who love Him as a caring, earthly father would look after his children. Struggles with difficult situations will bring spiritual strength, growth, and maturity into the lives of believers. He also says believers would become like Jesus by growing in maturity, faith, and hope, and this growth allows the believer to know something about themselves. The idea of joy in a spiritual maturity process is not only about happiness. It is also, more importantly, about spiritual growth in the life of the individual.

The evaluation on the Spiritual Maturity Assessment about joy is in question 1: "I rate the nine Fruit of the Spirit listed in Galatians 5:22–23 in my life as follows: (rate each fruit from 1–5: 1 = very weak; 5 = very strong)."

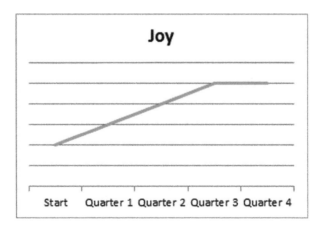

# Peace

The word translated in the New Testament as peace was common in some forms of greeting or farewell. Examples can be found in Luke 10:5, Galatians 6:16, James 2:16, and John 20:19; 1 Corinthians 7:15 references peace in the home. It is also used to indicate a cessation of conflict, as found in Luke 14:32, Acts 12:20, Romans 14:19, and Ephesians 4:3.

The Hebrew word most recognized as peace is *shalom*. The difficulty with relying on *shalom* as a description for peace is the number of times it is identified with different meanings. The translators for the New International Version of the Bible used *shalom* in seventy different ways. Therefore, it is better to look for a definition of peace rather than a translation of a word, and one of the best descriptions of the word *peace* is found in John 14:27 (HCAB): "Peace I leave with you. My peace I give to you. I do not give to you as the world gives. Your heart must not be troubled or fearful."

The peace Jesus gave to the apostles is a feature of life for someone who walks with God in a positive relationship.[34] Peace, as one of the Fruit of the Spirit, may literally mean individuals who have a countenance of being comfortable with the presence of God in their life.

The evaluation on the Spiritual Maturity Assessment about peace is in question 1: "I rate the nine Fruit of the Spirit listed in Galatians 5:22–23 in my life as follows: (rate each fruit from 1–5: 1 = very weak; 5 = very strong)."

---

[34] Carpenter, E. E., & Comfort, P. W. (2000). In *Holman Treasury of key Bible words: 200 Greek and 200 Hebrew words defined and explained* (p. 135). Nashville, TN: Broadman & Holman Publishers.

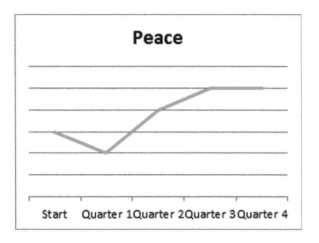

**Peace**

Start    Quarter 1  Quarter 2  Quarter 3  Quarter 4

## Patience

The most common concept of patience has been described as not becoming upset quickly and slow to become angry. Paul writing to the church in Rome instructs them to be patient. In Romans 5:3–4 Paul instructs them to rejoice in the trials and problems brought to them because of their faith in Christ, because the trials and problems will bring forth patience and patience produces a proven character which in turn brings the individual into hope.

The concept of patience in the disciple-making process is for the one being discipled to exhibit a calm spirit even in the face of adversity. It does not imply a "milk-toast" type lifestyle. If there are negative things happening around you, face them with courage and address the situation in a calm manner.

The evaluation on the Spiritual Maturity Assessment about patience is in question 1: "I rate the nine Fruit of the Spirit listed in Galatians 5:22–23 in my life as follows: (rate each fruit from 1–5: 1 = very weak; 5 = very strong)."

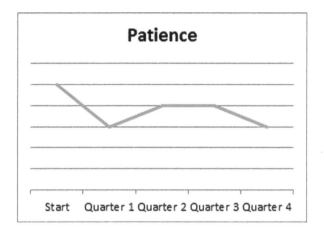

## Kindness

Kindness is an attitude, an action, and an emotion. It is an attitude represented by a spirit willing to help people, even if you do not have a good relationship with them. It is an action when you are compelled to help someone who has demonstrated a need. It is an emotion when you experience a favorable reaction from the one you have helped. The action of helping does not have to be a huge or difficult thing to undertake. It can be a soft-spoken word, a pat on the back, or opening a door.

I had an experience a few years ago that positively impacts me today. A woman has been attending our church for a couple of years. She does not enter the worship center but sits in the welcome center without speaking to anyone. A few months after I noticed her, I simply walked near her and said, "Hello." She did not respond or acknowledge me in any way. I did not let that deter me but verbally greeted her each Sunday I was at church.

After about six months as I passed by her and greeted her, I was astonished when she replied, "Hello." This continued for a few months. One Sunday when I greeted her, she extended her hand to shake hands and greeted me. Now when I greet her, she usually stands up and walks over to me to greet me. During the course of a year, I have experienced an attitude of kindness, an action of kindness, and an emotion of kindness.

The evaluation on the Spiritual Maturity Assessment about kindness is in question 1: "I rate the nine Fruit of the Spirit listed in Galatians 5:22–23 in my life as follows: (rate each fruit from 1–5: 1 = very weak; 5 = very strong)."

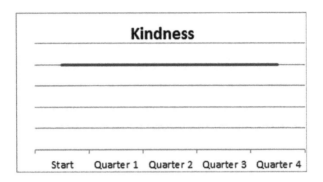

## Goodness

Goodness in man is not a mere passive quality, but it is the deliberate preference of right over wrong, the firm and persistent resistance of all moral evil, and the choosing and following of all moral good.[35] In everything we do, the temptation to cut a corner, to tell a "little white lie," or to cut someone down in order to make ourselves look better is present. Someone who wants to exhibit the Fruit of the Spirit will not be immune from the opportunity of selecting the glamor of evil over the joy of doing good. It does not matter your station in life, the vocation you are pursuing, or your relationship to Christ. We all are faced with these temptations throughout our life. Exhibiting this element of the Fruit of the Spirit is not being immune from the choices. Goodness is in right over wrong. "We are reminded that the Christian life in its truth is likeness to God, the source and

---

[35] Easton, M. G. (1893). In *Easton's Bible dictionary*. New York: Harper & Brothers.

perfection of all good. 2 Thess 1:11 regards God Himself as expressing His goodness in and through us."[36]

The evaluation on the Spiritual Maturity Assessment about goodness is in question 1: "I rate the nine Fruit of the Spirit listed in Galatians 5:22–23 in my life as follows: (rate each fruit from 1–5: 1 = very weak; 5 = very strong)."

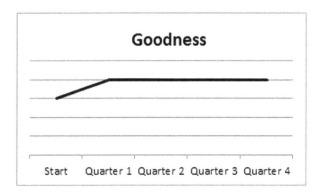

## Faithfulness

"Throughout the Scriptures faith is the trustful human response to God's self-revelation via His words and His actions."[37] In today's culture, faithfulness is thought of as an allegiance or a strong sense of duty. Other English words (i.e., *strengthen, support, consistency, trustworthiness,* and *uphold*) can be used in this characteristic and be just as definitive. The human characteristic that is desirable in trying to understand the Fruit of the Spirit is trustworthiness. If a person wants to be a disciple of Christ and exhibit the Fruit of the Spirit, trustworthiness should be one of the first things that is recognized in

---

[36] Walker, W. L. (1915). Goodness. In J. Orr, J. L. Nuelsen, E. Y. Mullins, & M. O. Evans (Eds.), *The International Standard Bible Encyclopedia* (Vol. 1–5, p. 1279). Chicago: The Howard-Severance Company.

[37] Parks, D. M. (2003). Faith, Faithfulness. In C. Brand, C. Draper, A. England, S. Bond, E. R. Clendenen, & T. C. Butler (Eds.), *Holman Illustrated Bible Dictionary* (p. 547). Nashville, TN: Holman Bible Publishers.

that person's life. A trustworthy person will follow through with the things Jesus has called us to do. This is especially true of pastors and other ministers. Timothy George wrote,

> As an aspect of the fruit of the Spirit, *pistis* has yet a further meaning: faithfulness, fidelity, that is, the quality of being true, trustworthy, and reliable in all one's dealings with others. For those who are called to serve as leaders of God's people, now as then, faithfulness should be a far more coveted mark of ministry than temporal success, ecclesiastical recognition, or popular acclaim.[38]

A trustworthy individual will seek to be an example of what it means to be a disciple of Christ. In 1 John 1:9 (NVC), it states Jesus is faithful (trustworthy) to fulfill what He promised: "But if we confess our sins, he will forgive our sins, because we can trust God to do what is right. He will cleanse us from all the wrongs we have done." We should strive to be like Jesus.

The evaluation on the Spiritual Maturity Assessment about faithfulness is in question 1: "I rate the nine Fruit of the Spirit listed in Galatians 5:22–23 in my life as follows: (rate each fruit from 1–5: 1 = very weak; 5 = very strong)."

---

[38] George, T. (1994). *Galatians* (Vol. 30, pp. 403–404). Nashville: Broadman & Holman Publishers.

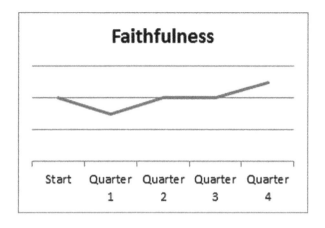

## Gentleness

A gentle nature does not necessarily mean a meek and mild personality. The word to describe a gentle attitude is *mercy*. There is no translation directly from the Greek language for *mercy*. A former pastor once said the meaning of mercy is "to get inside of." Another way of stating the meaning is experiencing things with another person by knowing exactly what he or she is going through.

Jesus's response to Peter's question about forgiveness in Matthew 18:22 is an example of mercy. Peter asked Jesus how many times he must forgive a person. Peter's expectation was of the traditional number of times, seven times, to forgive. Jesus's response went beyond what Peter thought Jesus would say. Many times, when we read this passage, we focus on the seventy times seven number and forget the message behind the numbers. Jesus was presenting the concept of mercy versus law.

When I was growing up on a farm the time came to "break a colt," the term used then for training a young horse to be ridden. I sat on the corral fence and watched as my uncle went through the exercise. The common thought of the day was to break the colt's free spirit and have him become tame. My uncle had other ideas. The colt was small, and my uncle was tall. He straddled the colt and still had his feet on the ground. As the colt walked around the corral, every once in a while, my uncle would lower his weight onto the back of the colt. The colt would instantly start to buck. My uncle would simply stand up and continue to walk while staying on top of the colt.

In just a short amount of time, the colt accepted the weight of a human on his back. His spirit was not broken, but he would allow someone to ride him. I ought to know. He became my horse. We had some good times; however, once in a while his free spirit would kick in, and we would really have some fun times.

A gentle spirit comes from the love of God and not religious traditions. Let the one being discipled see the mercy side of Christianity rather than only seeing the legal side of Christianity.

The evaluation on the Spiritual Maturity Assessment about gentleness is in question 1: "I rate the nine Fruit of the Spirit listed in Galatians 5:22–23 in my life as follows: (rate each fruit from 1–5: 1 = very weak; 5 = very strong)."

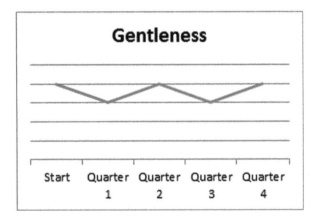

## Self-control

In his second letter, Peter presented a list of qualities a disciple is to exhibit. He begins with faith and lists seven additional qualities concluding with love. Peter then follows the list with a reason for engaging each of these qualities: "For if these qualities are yours and are increasing, they will keep you from being useless or unfruitful in the knowledge of our Lord Jesus Christ."[39] If we put all of these qualities into action, we will be fruitful and useful. The midpoint of the list of qualities is self-control. The idea expressed in 2 Peter is to live a life under control, sensible or prudent. The idea established a suggestion of a life that is measured restraint in all things.

The evaluation on the Spiritual Maturity Assessment about self-control is in question 1: "I rate the nine Fruit of the Spirit listed in Galatians 5:22–23 in my life as follows: (rate each fruit from 1–5: 1 = very weak; 5 = very strong)."

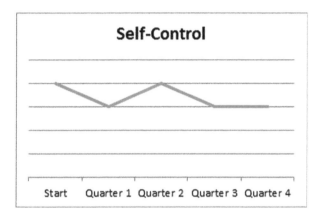

## Prayer

We had a series of cottage prayer meetings in preparation for a revival while my wife, Marlene, and I were serving at our first full-time ministry position. I had grown up in a Christian home and had been a Christian for several years. The concept of prayer was nothing new to me: asking God for what you needed and thanking Him for what He has given you. The pastor gave me the assignment of organizing the cottage prayer meetings and selecting the curriculum.

---

[39] *The Holy Bible: Holman Christian standard version.* (2009). (2 Peter 1:8). Nashville: Holman Bible Publishers.

A friend recommended the book *Prayer: Conversing with God* by Rosalind Rinker. The title sounded interesting, and reading it, I decided this concept of prayer was something our church members needed to explore. Rosalind Rinker's book became the curriculum for the cottage prayer meetings. The basic gist of the book is prayer should not be a formalized, rigid, patterned, and one-sided presentation. Prayer should generally be a warm, spontaneous conversation between you and God.

Through the experience of the book and the conversations during the cottage prayer meetings, I experienced a noticeable change in my approach to prayer. The idea of a conversation rather than a petition was the main ingredient of change. The Baker Encyclopedia of the Bible provides a clear statement about prayer: "It is not to inform God of matters that he would otherwise be ignorant of, and the validity of prayer is not affected by length or repetitiveness. (Matthew 6:5–15)."[40] A person who is part of a disciple-making process should begin to sense a closeness with God during sessions of prayer.

The questions on the Spiritual Maturity Assessment that relate to prayer are

> 5 "I spend time in prayer on a daily basis."
> 12 "When I pray, I pray more for others than for myself."
> 20 "Prayer is a worship experience for me."
> 28 "When I pray, I spend more time "in prayer" than I did in the past."
> 31 "I desire to help other Christians share their faith."

---

[40] Elwell, W. A., & Beitzel, B. J. (1988). Prayer. In *Baker encyclopedia of the Bible* (Vol. 2, p. 1746). Grand Rapids, MI: Baker Book House.

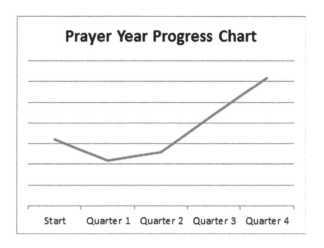

## Bible Reading

The textbook for life is the Bible. The textbook for the church is the Bible. The textbook for disciple-making is the Bible. Reading the Bible is a must for an individual desiring to become a spiritually maturing person. Bible reading as part of the disciple-making process is Scripture reading for personal development in addition to reading the Bible in preparing to attend or teach a Bible study group.

Reading the Bible as a personal exercise will allow the individual to develop a sense of God to reveal His power and direction in that individual's life rather than reading the Bible in preparation for another event. Many pastors and church leaders are beginning to realize our Bible study programs are producing students and not disciples. A person wishing to experience spiritual growth should be willing to continue or start a personal daily Bible-reading plan.

The questions on the Spiritual Maturity Assessment that relate to Bible reading are

> 3 "I read my Bible on a daily basis."
> 11 "My Bible reading is more devotional than it is 'study.'"
> 18 "I attempt to memorize Bible verses at least once per month."

26 "Realizing that my strength, hope, meaning and purpose are found in God's Word, I read the Bible as a searcher."

33 "I find myself referring to my Bible readings as I have conversations with others."

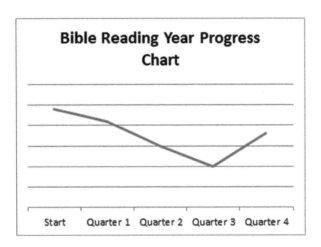

## Community—Church

Churches are often referred to as religious organizations. This description is unfortunate because a church is more than an organization. A church is a community comprised of a group of persons gathered together for a particular purpose. In order to function as a church, some type of organizational structure must be present.

However, at the heart of the church is not the organizational structure but people. The community is made up of people who are loved by God. The church that holds organization and structure to be more important than people has lost sight of the meaning of the Gospel. God's connection with mankind is shown through God's interaction with people such as Adam and Eve, Abraham, Moses, David, Jesus, and the apostles.

It is through the interaction with God and these people, as well as many others, we can see God's love and concern, His counsel and

His discipline, and a return to His love and guidance. The community called church should continue this interaction. It must be stated one more time. Organization and structure are important for a church to function, but it is people that are most important to God. People who wish to see spiritual growth should seek to understand how God wants them to function in His community.

The questions on the Spiritual Maturity Assessment that relate to community are:

> 6 "I attend worship at my church every Sunday I am in town."
>
> 9 "I attend my Bible study group provided by my church every week I am in town."
>
> 16 "I have built spiritually healthy relationships with fellow members of my church family."
>
> 23 "I allow at least one person to hold me accountable as a believer in Jesus Christ."
>
> 29 "It is important to me that I be a spiritual mentor to another person."

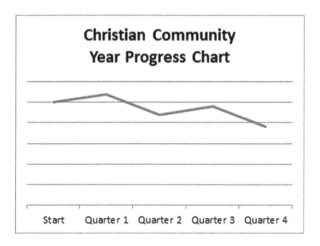

63

# Stewardship

Stewardship is the receiving, managing, and distribution of resources. When the topic of discussion is stewardship, many people will focus on finances. Stewardship is more than finances. The term also encompasses objects such as houses, furniture, property, and clothes. Stewardship also relates to time and talent management. Everything we touch in life has a stewardship component. The farmer must be a good steward of the land, or he will not have crops to harvest. The manufacturer must be a good steward of the inventory in order to have products to sell. The teacher must be a good steward of the students so the students can find fulfillment beyond school.

Before we examine the three actions of stewardship, we must realize we do not own anything—it is all God's. He is just allowing us to use some of His things in order for us to have a sustainable life on earth. Some would counter with the statement "I own my house. I am paying for it." The problem with that line of thinking is it does not go back far enough. Where did the building materials for the house come from? Who pulled the raw material from the ground or felled the tree? If we take any item back far enough, the only answer would be, "It came from God." A person who is desiring to grow spiritually should work through the ownership concept. If we can agree that God owns it all, the distribution process will look different from what we thought.

The three actions of stewardship are receiving, managing, and distributing resources. Receiving resources comes from all directions in all forms. Some resources are earned as salary. Some resources are gifts we received. Some resources are acquired because we bought something or sold something. Resources come to us from many different avenues. Managing resources depends on who is in control. If we try to be in control of our life, the resources will be used based on our desires, dreams, and marketing ploys. With God in control, He will guide us in how we are to distribute our resources. God's plan will be better than our plan because He sees all and knows all. He can see what is in the future and helps us have things and enjoy things. People who wish to be spiritually growing will be willing to give God's things back to God and let Him guide them in their use of our resources.

The questions on the Spiritual Maturity Assessment that relate to stewardship are

> 7 "I am a tither to my local church."
>
> 14 "I am an active volunteer in the life of my church."
>
> 27 "I gladly support God's work in our world with my finances."
>
> 32 "I verbally encourage others to participate in God's kingdom with their finances and their service."

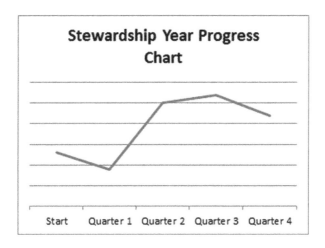

## Sharing Faith

In chapter 3, the position of disciple-making and evangelism is discussed. The Great Commission focuses on the total process of disciple-making, and evangelism is a part of that process. An e-mail was circulated with the lead statement boldly proclaiming, "Evangelism and discipleship are two sides of the same coin." That phrase sounds good, but I think it is not correct. Discipleship (disciple-making) is much broader than evangelism. It is Bible reading, engaging in a community of believers called the church, stewardship, prayer, and evangelism.

A friend made a statement that may clarify the issue. He said evangelism is the by-product of a maturing disciple. A maturing disciple will be more engaged in evangelism than a church member who is being told to be an evangelist in order to demonstrate their maturity in Christ. Since sharing one's faith is part of the maturity development process, it has been included as part of the assessment. You cannot be a maturing Christian without sharing your faith somewhere along the journey; however, you can be an evangelist without being a maturing Christian.

The questions on the Spiritual Maturity Assessment that relate to sharing your faith are

> 4 "I regularly share with others how I came to faith in Jesus Christ."
>
> 13 "I am willing to share what I believe about Jesus Christ with others during my daily routines and conversations."
>
> 19 "I have written out my faith story so that when I tell it, it is clear and easily understood by others."
>
> 25 "I have a strong desire to see other people come to believe in the saving power of Jesus Christ."
>
> 31 "I desire to help other Christians share their faith."

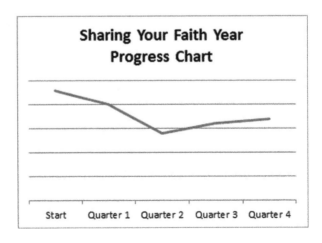

Sharing Your Faith Year Progress Chart

Start    Quarter 1    Quarter 2    Quarter 3    Quarter 4

## Foundations

The topics of belief about God, Jesus, the Bible, baptism, worship, and service are gathered together under the heading of "Foundations." Some areas listed under "Foundations" may also be in other segments of the assessment.

## God

God is the father of all creation and has a long history of interacting with His creations. He is a living, loving Supreme Being who deeply cares for His creations, as evidenced in Psalm 50:10 (cattle on a thousand hills), Matthew 10:30 (hairs on your head being numbered), and John 19:16 (Jesus on the cross). God not only cared for those who lived in ages past, but He also cares for those who are alive today and those who will be coming in the future. God also expects His children to observe a higher standard of living than the rest of the world. Examples of God's desire to have His children exhibit a higher standard of living is shown in Exodus 20 (the Ten Commandments).

The questions on the Spiritual Maturity Assessment about God are

17 "I believe that God is the Creator of all things including human life and eternal life."
22 "I understand that God has a role and purpose for my life in the mission and ministry of my church."

## Jesus

Jesus came to earth as a baby that was born of a virgin. He established a new covenant between God and man through His sinless life, death on the cross, and resurrection. In the thirty-three years Jesus was in human form, He changed the thinking of mankind about how to perceive religions, how to relate to one another, how to worship God, how to disciple people, how to teach people, and how to come into the presence of God.

The question on the Spiritual Maturity Assessment about Jesus is 24: "I believe that Jesus was God in the flesh and He came to earth for the redemption of mankind."

## Bible

The Bible is a collection of interactions between God and man. God led a variety of people to write, dictate, or share stories, information, genealogies, lessons, poems, and sayings that were collected into sixty-six books. Even though a number of people created the words that are on the pages of the Bible and many more people were the subjects of the stories, there is one theme carried across all sixty-six books: the story of God's interaction with man.

The question on the Spiritual Maturity Assessment about the Bible is 10: "I believe the Bible is divinely inspired and is God's revelation of Himself to man."

## Baptism

A debate is occurring in religious circles that revolves around whether baptism is a sacrament or an ordinance. Ben Witherington states, "We must keep one thing in mind, a person's theology of baptism is, to one degree or another, a function of a person's soteriology—one's theology of salvation."[41] If an individual believes a person must be baptized in order for the salvation process to be completed, then the individual believes baptism is a sacrament. If baptism is only a symbol of what has already taken place on the inside of the person, then the individual believes baptism is an ordinance.

The term *baptism* generally refers "to dip" or "immerse." Baptism did not originate with John the Baptizer. It was a common practice throughout the known world as a process of purification. One group of people broke away from Jerusalem to establish their own process in preparing for the coming of the Messiah. The group

---

[41] Ben Witherington, *Troubled Waters Rethinking the Theology of Baptism* (Waco: Baylor University Press, 2007), 113.

was the Essenes, who located their following in the area at Quorum, where the Dead Sea Scrolls were located, in the twentieth century.

"More than a half dozen *mikvaoth* were found at Quorum, serving a community of only about 200 Essenes. Moreover, the *Rule of the Community* contains regulations regarding the practice of ritual purification among the Covenanters. Evidently, the Essenes were a messianic 'baptist,' reformation sect of Jews who had protested the corruption of the Jerusalem temple cults by retreating to the northeast shore of the Dead Sea there to immerse their community in preparation for the coming of the Messiah. John the Baptizer, as the Fourth Gospel refers to him, also had apparently retreated to the wilderness to form a messianic 'baptist' reformation sect immersing the people of God in preparation for the coming of the Messiah. The fact that his movement was centered only about a mile or so from Quorum makes it difficult to believe that there should have been no connection between them."[42]

Before John the Baptizer made his appearance, two types of baptism were practiced: purification process baptism and Jewish proselyte baptism. Both types of baptism used the immersion method and both types of baptism were self-administered. The Essenes established a third type of baptism, which was done by immersion but was not self-administered. The Essenes baptism was a baptism of repentance from the corrupt dealings of the Jewish religion in the temple government. The Essenes wanted to demonstrate their change of heart away from man-corrupted religion to a God-led life. When John the Baptizer made his appearance, as shown in Matthew 3, and called for repentance, it was not the repentance from sin to God. Instead, it was a turning to God in preparation for the coming of the Messiah.

The one question left to be answered is how John became attached to the Essenes. Ben Witherington was able to provide one possibility. Witherington suggests that John, like so many others, was sent to Quorum to learn and be indoctrinated with the desert disci-

---

[42] Shurden, Alter B., *Baptist Vision Baptism & Lord's Supper*, (Macon: Smyth & Helwys Publishing, 1999), 96-97.

pline of the community. This might have been done at the time of the death of his parents.[43]

The question on the Spiritual Maturity Assessment about baptism is 36: "I believe baptism was illustrated by Jesus' baptism and is a visible depiction of what has taken place in the spiritual life of a new believer."

## Worship

Worship originally referred to humans expressing homage to God. In the culture of today, it generally refers to an activity or event conducted by a religious body. The worship services of the church today appear to focus on what the people in the room can do for or offer to God rather than celebrating what God has done for us and for the human race. Many of the songs used during worship services have the theme of who God is, whereas songs of the church in previous times focused on what God has done. The Scripture reminds us "the Son of Man did not come to be served, but to serve."[44]

There should be a time within the worship service to allow individuals to have personal time to give God adoration, thanksgiving, or special prayers. If there is no time allotted for personal experiences during the worship service, the disciple-making process should provide suggestions about private worship times at home, etc. A person wishing to be a part of a disciple-making process should want to experience personal worship on a regular basis.

The question on the Spiritual Maturity Assessment about worship is 6: "I attend worship at my church every Sunday I am in town."

## Service

Service in the context of the disciple-making process is the willingness of the individual to participate in a church ministry or

---

[43] Witherington, *Troubled Waters Rethinking the Theology of Baptism*, 26.
[44] *The Holy Bible: Holman Christian standard version.* (2009). (Mk 10:45). Nashville: Holman Bible Publishers.

activity other than the worship service or Bible-study program. No set number of ministries or extracurricular activities a church should conduct is required. That is a decision for each church. However, it would be wise for the church, at a point in time determined by the church leadership, to consider conducting a ministry and activity audit.

In 1999 the deacons of a church decided to evaluate the ministry of the deacon body. It was a traditional group focusing on administrative affairs rather than ministry opportunities. Following several months of examination and discussion, the members of the deacon body voted to eliminate all administrative activity conducted by the deacon body. Their reasoning was sound and wise. They stated that the church had committees, groups, and church staff members who were assigned the administrative responsibilities that the deacon body were doing. They also voted to define the work of the deacon body to be ministry focused group, and they defined six ministries the deacons would develop and execute as a ministry plan.

In 2017, the deacon body was scheduled to have eighty-nine active deacons and was still doing the same six ministries. In order to engage more of the active deacons they were divided into seventeen ministry teams. That year was a great year of seeing deacon participation and hearing ministry reports.

An individual who wishes to participate in a disciple-making process should desire to be an active part in one of the church ministries or a leader in a church program. A word of caution: If possible, do not overload an individual with more than one ministry or church program assignment. Let the individual choose the ministries and/or programs in which they wish to participate.

The question on the Spiritual Maturity Assessment about Service is 14: "I am an active volunteer in the life of my church."

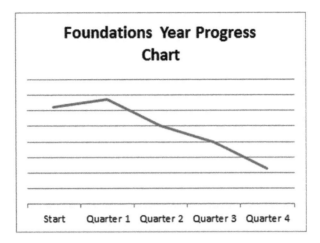

# CHAPTER 7

## How to Use the Assessment

The Spiritual Maturity Assessment is a questionnaire to be administered to an individual or to several individuals in an ongoing group like a Bible study group. The assessment is to be administered multiple times across an established time period of at least two months. The evaluation of each administration of the assessment is to be done as a confidential meeting between the individual who completed the questionnaire and an assigned mentor.

If an organized group is selected to participate in the assessment process, the administrator of the spiritual maturity organization is to make a presentation to the entire group concerning the assessment. Following the presentation, the members of the group are to indicate if they wish to participate. Those who indicate their desire to participate in the assessment will then receive a contact from a mentor with additional information relating to how the mentoring meetings will be conducted. All mentoring meetings are confidential, and the mentor is to guide the participant in interpreting the information from the assessment. It is normal for less than one half of the members of a group to participate during the first use of the assessment. It is better for a smaller number of the group to participate than to have a majority of the group say they will participate but drop out quickly. The assessment can be offered to the group at a later time for those who did not participate during the first opportunity.

If the disciple-making team decides to open the assessment to individuals, a promotional program should be developed to dispense information about the assessment to church members. A signup process should be made available to allow individual members to indicate an interest in the assessment so a mentor can schedule a meeting with them.

Following each administration of the assessment, the mentor is to take the completed assessment sheets to the disciple-making input person. The input person is to enter the information from the assessment sheets into the assessment tally sheet. The input person will print two copies of the charts generated by the tally sheet. Both copies of the charts are to be given to the mentor who will give one copy to the individual who completed the assessment sheets. The mentor will use the charts to allow the individual to interpret, with a few comments from the mentor, the meaning of the charts to the individual. After the meeting with the individual, the mentor will make notes about the meeting and attach them to the charts. The notes and charts will be returned to the input person, to be placed in a secure area in the church office. The mentor will retrieve the notes following the next administration of the assessment.

The only other person to gain access to the notes and charts is the disciple-making administrator. From time to time throughout the assessment process, the administrator will develop a general summary of the information gathered from the notes and charts. These summaries may be given to the leader of a group if the assessment is being used in an established group. The administrator is to give a summary report to the pastor on a regular basis. At no time are individuals to be identified in any summary report.

The assessment found in appendix C of this book may be copied for use in the church or an electronic copy of the assessment may be obtained from Cornerstone Consultants LLC. The assessment tally sheet may be obtained from Cornerstone Consultants LLC at www.cornerstoneconsultants.org.

# CHAPTER 8

## *Questions and Answers*

*T*he main focus of this work is to direct you to a process of measuring spiritual maturity. In order to get to the measurement information, several items of background were presented. Everything we do or say should be built on a solid foundation. The importance of why a measurement process is important would have been missed if the measurement tool was the first thing presented in the book.

In the process of developing the material for this book, several questions were asked as people inquired about our work or were contacted to provide information. The following questions may provide additional insight concerning the Measuring Spiritual Maturity process.

## Question 1: Why do we need a measurement tool? We have never had one before.

There are three reasons for having a measurement tool. First, things have changed dramatically in the past thirty to forty years. In the past, when a particular word was said, we understood what it meant. Today, there could be three to four meanings of that same word. It is more complex today. The complexity should drive us to look for tools we can use to better understand what is happening in the spiritual lives of the people God has called us to lead.

Second, many church leaders today look for churches that seem to be "making it" and try to emulate what they are doing. It is wise for church leaders to examine the ministries and programs of other churches. However, the question the church leaders need to be asking is not how to add the ministry or program to their church, but is the ministry or program correct for our church? Simply picking up someone else's idea and dropping it into your list of activities without alteration may not be a wise idea.

Third, a definitive measurement to indicate if a person is progressing, regressing, or standing still in their spiritual life should be in place. The main indicator of spiritual growth in many churches is attendance. Attendance is not a viable indicator because of the variables. So many things will affect attendance: weather, vacations, family crisis, holidays, dissatisfaction, relocation, and illness, to name a few things.

Church statistics shown in the 2010 US Religion Census for 235 religious denominations and religious groups indicate only 21% of the 150,686,156 members, children, and other attenders participated in worship services. An additional study of the 2017 statistics of a state in a Baptist denomination was conducted, revealing only 30% of the 44,913 members attended worship and 19% of the members attended the ongoing Bible study program. American churches seem to be doing a poor job of disciple-making if attendance is the only indicator being recognized.

Additional information relating to this question may be found in chapter 3 of this work.

## Question 2: What are you really trying to do? You cannot measure spiritual maturity.

This question is partially true. Becoming spiritually mature is a spiritual event, not a physical event. If that is all we had to go by, it would be impossible to measure progress toward spiritual maturity. However, as with most things in life that are spiritual, there are physical actions within the spiritual concept that can be measured. The love a husband has for his wife and the wife for her husband is emotional and not physical. The way to exhibit love for a spouse is through physical actions: the giving of gifts, doing spontaneous activities to see the happiness and joy of the spouse, doing chores usually done by the spouse, and many other illustrations. A trained individual can study these physical activities and develop conclusions about the love between two people. Parents who want their children to succeed in life experience happiness or sadness toward the children because of what the children do. These acts of happiness or sadness cannot be measured, but the actions of the children can be measured, and a trained individual can determine the level of the emotional experience of the parents.

While the progress of an individual toward spiritual maturity cannot be measured, the actions in which an individual participates can be measured. These actions would include, but not be limited to, prayer, Bible reading, volunteer service in a church ministry, living out the Fruit of the Spirit (love, joy, peace, patience, kindness, goodness, faithfulness, gentleness, self-control), stewardship (time, talent, and finances), sharing of faith, church attendance, belief about God, belief about Jesus, belief about the Bible, belief about baptism, belief about worship. When these and other spiritual maturity actions are gathered and recorded, a trend line can be created indicating the spiritual progression of the individual. The progress may be growing toward maturity, growing away from maturity, or becoming static.

Additional information relating to this question may be found in chapter 4 of this work.

## Question 3: Why do we have to have a disciple-making process? I thought becoming a disciple was a part of becoming a Christian.

The answer to this question depends on the major element of *your* definition of a disciple. It is easy to accept another person's definition and implement it into the life of the church. That approach would be easy if all churches were exactly alike in belief, membership makeup, and leadership capabilities. All churches are not alike, so why do we take a generic approach to disciple-making?

Church leaders do not define disciple specifically for their church for a few specific reasons. Some churches are a part of a denominational structure that will not allow the individual church to develop concepts apart from the denomination. The material in this work does not denounce or support this form of church government. The reason the statement is placed at this point in the material is to state this is one of several reasons a church may not customize the definition of a disciple. Another reason a church may not have customized the definition of a disciple is that the church leaders have not been discipled themselves and therefore do not know how a disciple is to be defined. A third reason a church may not have customized the definition of a disciple is that no clear definition exists in the Christian world. Conversations revolving around discipleship can become very confusing because of the lack of a clear definition.

How are churches to create a customized definition of a disciple? The best way is to study the Gospels and identify what steps Jesus took to disciple the Twelve. A basic fact will need to be the focal point of the study. Disciple-making is not a single-step activity. A multistep disciple-making process is outlined in this work. However, it is not the only outline a search of the Gospels may reveal.

Additional information relating to this question may be found in chapter 4 of this work.

## Question 4: Who will benefit by seeing a visual depiction of spiritual growth?

First, church members will be beneficiaries of a visualized indication of their spiritual growth. Intentional actions toward disciple-making will allow church members to be more proactive in reaching and growing other people. The individual who completes the assessments and sees the charts that depict the direction of growth will benefit if someone is available to mentor the individual in the interpretation.

Second, the church staff will also benefit. The information gleaned from a disciple-making process could be beneficial for church staff members as they plan events, activities, and programs. Part of the plan outlined in this material suggests the identity of the individual participating in taking the assessments should remain confidential to everyone except the mentor assigned to the individual. However, the church staff might be allowed to see a summary of the charts without identifying individuals who participated in the assessments.

Third, the pastor will benefit by having additional information to consider as he outlines topics for future sermons and to give him another tool in the toolbelt to equip the saints. Part of being equippers of the saints is to intentionally guide them to experience spiritual growth. Spiritual growth will not necessarily be attained through attendance only. We are not to be making students. We are to be disciple-makers.

Fourth, church leaders will benefit by shifting their focus from ministry managers to equippers of church members. Robby Gallaty said during an interview in February 2018 with a writer from *Facts and Trends* Magazine, "The focus of church leaders must shift from being executors of ministry ourselves to being equippers of the saints, who will in turn partner with us to carry out the ministry. By doing so, people fulfill their God-given calling to participate in the good works, which God prepared ahead of time for us to do (Ephesians 2:10)."[45]

Fifth, the church will benefit when church members begin to recognize their spiritual abilities and use them in the development of the church. This may result in their willingness to be leaders, to attend more often, and allow guests who come to the church to see and recognize people who are interested in them.

Additional information relating to this question may be found in chapter 5 of this work.

## Question 5: Why does a spiritual maturity measurement assessment need to be administered several times?

Most of the spiritual growth inventories, or assessments, are designed to be administered only one time, and there are good reasons for having a one administration approach. Most people do not

---

[45] Robby Gallaty, Developing A Culture of Discipleship in Your Church, (Facts & Trends Magazine, Nashville: Lifeway Christian Resources, 2018).

like to take assessments and balk at taking an assessment more than once. This is a valid reason for a one or two administration process if the purpose of the assessment is aimed at the individual discovering things about themselves.

An assessment administered once or twice will only give a snapshot of the attitude and emotional state of the person taking the assessment. The assessment will yield a picture of how the individual feels about the topics contained in the assessment. If the same individual takes the assessment a month or a year later, the results would give a snapshot of the individual at the time the assessment was taken.

Very little can be interpreted from the assessment as to the progression toward spiritual maturity. When a person initially completes an assessment, there is a tendency to give responses based on what they perceive the examiner would like to hear. Also other factors in life can impact how a person will respond to questions on an assessment.

Measuring Spiritual Maturity is designed to allow individuals who participate in the assessments to recognize where their strengths and weaknesses are in their spiritual life. It is also designed for all church leaders to evaluate how they are doing in fulfilling Jesus's command to make disciples.

Measuring Spiritual Maturity recommends between four and six administrations of the assessment across three months, six months, nine months, or twelve months. After the second or third administration, most people will be responding to the questions as they see the questions relate to their lives. Measuring Spiritual Maturity also provides a support network of mentors to guide the participants in evaluating each completed assessment. The mentor program is not designed for the mentor to tell the individual the results or suggest what should be done. A mentor is a guide.

Additional information relating to this question may be found in chapter 2 of this work.

## Question 6: Do we have to do everything as it is presented in this book?

The short answer is no, you do not have to do everything exactly as it is presented in this book. It would be nearly impossible to write material that would fit every church exactly as it is written. Churches, or religious organizations, have the freedom to craft the process to fit their organization, doctrinal beliefs, and schedules.

However, a couple of items are critical to the process. First, the multiple administrations provide more important information to evaluate the disciple-making process. If you wish to shorten the time of administrations, it is recommended to allow at least three weeks between administrations. Second, the concept of enlisting multiple mentors is not as critical as the time between administrations. It is important to have someone who is trained to assist those who take the assessments in evaluating the results. A smaller church may enlist and train one mentor, and a larger church may enlist and train several mentors. Third, the church may wish to use wording for the assessment that is better suited for your situation.

If you would like the wording of the assessment to be changed, send the redesigned assessment to randy@cornerstgoneconsultants.org. We will change the assessment and the tally sheet to fit your nomenclature.

Additional information relating to this question may be found in chapter 1 of this work.

## Question 7: Does Cornerstone Consultants Ministries LLC provide assistance to install and/or use the Measuring Spiritual Maturity process?

Yes, assistance is available. Contact Cornerstone Consultants Ministries LLC, either by using the e-mail address listed above or going to cornerstoneconsultants.org website. Assistance can be customized to meet your needs. Some of the options are a telephone consultation, an electronic video consultation, or an onsite consultation. Cornerstone Consultants Ministries, LLC has conducted work in all fifty states.

# APPENDIX A

*Wilkins's Five Models of Discipleship*

| MODEL | STRENGTHS | WEAKNESSES |
|-------|-----------|------------|
| Disciples are learners | One who follows a great teacher. Places himself/herself under authority of a teacher without any reference to Christianity. This model emphasizes a variety of different kinds of followers who were called disciples. | The Greek term for *disciple* is used in Scripture in a manner different than simply to designate a *learner*. In the book of Acts, the term is generally used without any qualifiers simply to designate "Christians." |

| | | |
|---|---|---|
| Disciples are committed believers | A believer who has made a commitment to follow Jesus and obey His radical demands of discipleship. Emphasizes the count the cost concept of discipleship. It suggests there are two levels within the church today—disciples and ordinary believers. | This model may not take into consideration Jesus's discipleship messages and the spiritual nature of the audiences to whom he directs his messages. The two-group system of Christians presents a problematic concept of biblical discipleship. |
| Disciples are ministers | A believer who has been called out from among lay believers in order to enter into ministry. This model comes from observing the close relationship of the twelve disciples with Jesus and their later ministry. | Same difficulties as the second model, plus it does not observe the difference between the twelve disciples and the twelve apostles. |
| Disciples are converts; discipleship comes later | One who has been evangelized and later processes growth. A disciple is a believer. | This model separates the imperative of the Great Commission, "make disciples," from "baptizing" and "teaching." |

| | | |
|---|---|---|
| Disciples are converts who are in the process of discipleship | A believer who enters the life of discipleship at the time of conversion. | This model does not always clarify which of the demands of discipleship given by Jesus were for whom, nor does it specify the purpose for the demands. This model confuses conversion and commitment. |

Wilkins, Michael. *Following the Master: A Biblical Theology of Discipleship*. Grand Rapids, MI: Zondervan, 1992.

# APPENDIX B

## *Spiritual Maturity Surveys Used For Research*

1. Discipleship Growth Review by Greg Laurie, Camarillo Community Church, Camarillo, California
2. Pathways to Glory Spiritual Growth Assessment by Harvey L. Diamond, Albuquerque, New Mexico
3. Pathways to Spiritual Growth by Central United Methodist Church, Fayetteville, Arkansas
4. Spiritual Growth Assessment Tool by New Birth Church, Charlotte, North Carolina
5. Spiritual Health Assessment by True Foundation, David and Sonya Cameron, Tacoma, Washington
6. Spiritual Assessment Inventory by Debra K. Burton. This survey was part of a dissertation at Liberty University in the Doctor of Philosophy in Professional Counseling.
7. Spiritual Growth Survey by Bill Gaultiere
8. Spiritual Growth Assessment Process by LifeWay Christian Resources
9. Spiritual Formation Inventory by Brad Waggoner
10. Stonemill Church Spiritual Growth Assessment
11. The Christian Life Profile Assessment Workbook by Randy Frazee
12. The Church Health Assessment by Sean Keith
13. The Spiritual Growth Assessment Tool by Fairhope United Methodist Church, Louisville, Ohio
14. Willow Creek Reveal Study

# APPENDIX C

## *The Assessment*

NAME _____ GROUP _____ DATE_____

    This personal assessment is for your use to gauge your own spiritual maturing progress. This is an assessment—not an opinion survey. This assessment will be helpful if you are honest in marking the responses. Do not answer what you wish the answer would be but what actually is the current answer for your life. Your assessment will be held in confidence between you and your mentor.

1.    I rate the nine Fruit of the Spirit listed in Galatians 5:22–23 in my life as follows: (Rate each fruit from 1–5: 1 = very weak; 5 = very strong)

       _____  **LOVE**
       _____  **JOY**
       _____  **PEACE**
       _____  **PATIENCE**
       _____  **KINDNESS**
       _____  **GOODNESS**
       _____  **FAITHFULNESS**
       _____  **GENTLENESS**
       _____  **SELF-CONTROL**

2.  I believe God established the church on Jesus Christ and it is composed of believers under His authority.
    **Strongly Agree - Agree – Slightly Agree - Undecided/ Neutral – Slightly Disagree - Disagree - Strongly Disagree**

3.  I read my Bible daily.
    **Strongly Agree - Agree – Slightly Agree - Undecided/ Neutral – Slightly Disagree - Disagree - Strongly Disagree**

4.  I regularly share with others how I came to faith in Jesus Christ.
    **Strongly Agree - Agree – Slightly Agree - Undecided/ Neutral – Slightly Disagree - Disagree - Strongly Disagree**

5.  I spend time in prayer daily.
    **Strongly Agree - Agree – Slightly Agree - Undecided/ Neutral – Slightly Disagree - Disagree - Strongly Disagree**

6.  I attend worship at my church every Sunday I am in town.
    **Strongly Agree - Agree – Slightly Agree - Undecided/ Neutral – Slightly Disagree - Disagree - Strongly Disagree**

7.  I am a tither to my local church.
    **Strongly Agree - Agree – Slightly Agree - Undecided/ Neutral – Slightly Disagree - Disagree - Strongly Disagree**

8.  I am having conversations with other believers about the Fruit of the Spirit.
    **Strongly Agree - Agree – Slightly Agree - Undecided/ Neutral – Slightly Disagree - Disagree - Strongly Disagree**

9.  I attend my Bible study group provided by my church every week I am in town.
    **Strongly Agree - Agree – Slightly Agree - Undecided/ Neutral – Slightly Disagree - Disagree - Strongly Disagree**

10. I believe the Bible is divinely inspired and is God's revelation of Himself to man.
    **Strongly Agree - Agree – Slightly Agree - Undecided/ Neutral – Slightly Disagree - Disagree - Strongly Disagree**

11. My Bible reading is more devotional than it is a "study."
    **Strongly Agree - Agree – Slightly Agree - Undecided/ Neutral – Slightly Disagree - Disagree - Strongly Disagree**

12. When I pray, I pray more for others than for myself.
    **Strongly Agree - Agree – Slightly Agree - Undecided/ Neutral – Slightly Disagree - Disagree - Strongly Disagree**

13. I am willing to share what I believe about Jesus Christ with others during my daily routines and conversations.
    **Strongly Agree - Agree – Slightly Agree - Undecided/ Neutral – Slightly Disagree - Disagree - Strongly Disagree**

14. I am an active volunteer in the life of my church.
    **Strongly Agree - Agree – Slightly Agree - Undecided/ Neutral – Slightly Disagree - Disagree - Strongly Disagree**

15. The weakest fruit is something I am willing to work with God to improve in my life.
    **Strongly Agree - Agree – Slightly Agree - Undecided/ Neutral – Slightly Disagree - Disagree - Strongly Disagree**

16. I have built spiritually healthy relationships with fellow members of my church family.
    **Strongly Agree - Agree – Slightly Agree - Undecided/ Neutral – Slightly Disagree - Disagree - Strongly Disagree**

17. I believe that God is the Creator of all things including human life and eternal life.
    **Strongly Agree - Agree – Slightly Agree - Undecided/ Neutral – Slightly Disagree - Disagree - Strongly Disagree**

18. I attempt to memorize Bible verses at least once per month.
**Strongly Agree - Agree – Slightly Agree - Undecided/
Neutral– Slightly Disagree - Disagree - Strongly Disagree**

19. I have written out my faith story so that when I tell it, it is clear and easily understood by others.
**Strongly Agree - Agree – Slightly Agree - Undecided/
Neutral – Slightly Disagree - Disagree - Strongly Disagree**

20. Prayer is a worship experience for me.
**Strongly Agree - Agree – Slightly Agree - Undecided/
Neutral – Slightly Disagree - Disagree - Strongly Disagree**

21. My family and friends can easily observe the Fruit of the Spirit in my life.
**Strongly Agree - Agree – Slightly Agree - Undecided/
Neutral – Slightly Disagree - Disagree - Strongly Disagree**

22. I understand that God has a role and purpose for my life in the mission and ministry of my church.
**Strongly Agree - Agree – Slightly Agree - Undecided/
Neutral – Slightly Disagree - Disagree - Strongly Disagree**

23. I allow at least one person to hold me accountable as a believer in Jesus Christ.
**Strongly Agree - Agree – Slightly Agree - Undecided/
Neutral – Slightly Disagree - Disagree - Strongly Disagree**

24. I believe that Jesus was God in the flesh and He came to earth for the redemption of mankind.
**Strongly Agree - Agree – Slightly Agree - Undecided/
Neutral – Slightly Disagree - Disagree - Strongly Disagree**

25. I have a strong desire to see other people come to believe in the saving power of Jesus Christ.
   **Strongly Agree - Agree – Slightly Agree - Undecided/ Neutral – Slightly Disagree - Disagree - Strongly Disagree**

26. Realizing that my strength, hope, meaning, and purpose are found in God's Word, I read the Bible as a searcher.
   **Strongly Agree - Agree – Slightly Agree - Undecided/ Neutral – Slightly Disagree - Disagree - Strongly Disagree**

27. I gladly support God's work in our world with my finances.
   **Strongly Agree - Agree – Slightly Agree - Undecided/ Neutral – Slightly Disagree - Disagree - Strongly Disagree**

28. When I pray, I spend more time "in prayer" than I did in the past.
   **Strongly Agree - Agree – Slightly Agree - Undecided/ Neutral – Slightly Disagree - Disagree - Strongly Disagree**

29. It is important to me that I be a spiritual mentor to another person.
   **Strongly Agree - Agree – Slightly Agree - Undecided/ Neutral – Slightly Disagree - Disagree - Strongly Disagree**

30. I believe that all humans are sinners in need of salvation by Christ alone.
   **Strongly Agree - Agree – Slightly Agree - Undecided/ Neutral – Slightly Disagree - Disagree - Strongly Disagree**

31. I desire to help other Christians share their faith.
   **Strongly Agree - Agree – Slightly Agree - Undecided/ Neutral – Slightly Disagree - Disagree - Strongly Disagree**

32. I verbally encourage others to participate in God's kingdom with their finances and their service.
**Strongly Agree - Agree – Slightly Agree - Undecided/ Neutral – Slightly Disagree - Disagree - Strongly Disagree**

33. I find myself referring to my Bible readings as I have conversations with others.
**Strongly Agree - Agree – Slightly Agree - Undecided/ Neutral – Slightly Disagree - Disagree - Strongly Disagree**

34. My prayers are more about talking with God than asking God to provide things I need/want.
**Strongly Agree - Agree – Slightly Agree - Undecided/ Neutral – Slightly Disagree - Disagree - Strongly Disagree**

35. I believe it is the responsibility of every believer to grow in his/ her relationship with Christ.
**Strongly Agree - Agree – Slightly Agree - Undecided/ Neutral – Slightly Disagree - Disagree - Strongly Disagree**

36. I believe baptism was illustrated by Jesus's baptism and it is a visible depiction of what has taken place in the spiritual life of a new believer.
**Strongly Agree - Agree – Slightly Agree - Undecided/Neutral – Slightly Disagree - Disagree - Strongly Disagree[46]**

---

[46] You are given permission to copy the assessment from this book and use it in your discipling process. Please give acknowledgement that the development of this assessment was done by Dr. Randall H. Tompkins of Alexandria, Louisiana as part of the dissertation developed for the completion of the Doctor of Education Ministries Degree from Midwestern Baptist Theological Seminary. A project team of forty individuals was enlisted to assist in the development of the material.

# APPENDIX D

## *Bibliography*

### Books

Ambrose, Susan, Michael Bridges, Michele DiPietro, Marsha Lovett, Marie Norman, and Richard Mayer. *How Learning Works: Seven Research-based Principles for Smart Teaching.* San Francisco: John Wiley and Sons, 2010.

Balswick, Jack O., Pamela E. King, and Kevin S. Reimer. *The Reciprocating Self: Human Development in Theological Perspective.* Downer's Grove, IL: IVP Academic, 2005.

Bean, John, and Maryellen Weimer. *Engaging Ideas: The Professor's Guide to Integrating Writing, Critical Thinking, and Active Learning in the Classroom.* San Francisco: Jossey-Bass, 2011.

Blackaby, Henry, Richard Blackaby. *Moving People on to God's Agenda: Spiritual Leadership.* Nashville, TN: B & H Publishing Group, 2001.

Bergler, Thomas E. *Discipleship Essentials.* Downers Grove, IL: InterVarsity, 2014.

_____. *From Here to Maturity: Overcoming the Juvenilization of American Christianity.* Grand Rapids, MI: William B Eerdmans, 2014.

Blevins, Dean Gray, Mark Maddox. *Discovering Discipleship: Dynamics of Christian Education.* Kansas City, Mo: Beacon Hill, 2013.

Bridges, William. *Managing Transitions: Making the Most of Change.* Cambridge: DeCapo Press, 2009.

Bright, Bill. *Handbook for Christian Maturity: Bible Study (Ten Basic Steps Toward Christian Maturity)*. Colorado Springs, CO: New Life Publications, 1994.

Brookfield, Stephen, and Stephen Preskill. *Discussion as a Way of Teaching: Tools and Techniques for Democratic Classrooms*. San Francisco: Jossey-Bass, 2005.

Buckingham, Marcus. *Standout*. Nashville, TN: Thomas Nelson, 2011.

Collins, Jim. *Good to Great*. New York: HarperCollins Publishers, 2001.

Estep, James. *A Theology of Christian Education*, 320. Nashville, TN: Nashville: B and H Publishing Group, 2008.

Frazee, Randy. *The Christian Life Profile*. Grand Rapids, MI: Zondervan, 2005.

Geiger, Eric, Michael Kelley. *Transformational Discipleship: How People Really Grow*. Nashville, TN: B & H Publishing Group, 2012.

Hull, Bill. *The Disciple-making Pastor: Leading Others on the Journey of Faith*. Grand Rapids, MI: Baker Books, 2007.

Hutson, Lester. *Christian Maturity: Applying God's Principles for Spiritual Growth*. Houston, TX: Lester Hutson, 2014.

Kagan, Spencer. *Kagan Cooperative Learning*. San Clemente CA: Kagan Cooperative Learning, 2009.

Kouzes, James, and Barry Posner. *Leadership Challenge: How to Make Extraordinary Things Happen in Organizations*. San Francisco, Ca: Leadership Challenge, 2012.

LeFever, Marlene. *Learning Styles: Reaching Everyone God Gave You*. Colorado Springs: David C. Cook Publishing, 2004.

Malphurs, Aubrey. *Advanced Strategic Planning: A New Model for Church and Ministry Leaders, 2nd ed.* Grand Rapids, MI: Baker Books, 2005.

_____. *Building Leaders: Blueprints for Developing Leadership at Every Level of Your Church*. Grand Rapids, MI: Baker Books, 2004.

_____. *Developing a Vision for Ministry in the 21st Century*. Grand Rapids: Baker Publishing Group, 1999.

_____. *Look Before You Lead*. Grand Rapids: Baker Publishing Group, 2013.

_____. *Strategic Disciple Making: A Practical Tool for Successful Ministry*. Grand Rapids: Baker Books, 2009.

Mancini, Will. *Church Unique*. San Francisco: Jossey-Bass, 2008.

Meadows, Donella. *Thinking in Systems: A Primer*. White River Junction: Chelsa Green Publishing, 2008.

Meier, Dave. *The Accelerated Learning Handbook: A Creative Guide to Designing and Delivering Faster, More Effective Training Programs*. New York: McGraw Hill, 2000.

Melick, Rick. *Teaching That Transforms*. Nashville, TN: B and H Academic, 2010.

Ogden, Greg. *Discipleship Essentials: A Guide to Building Your Life in Christ*. Downers Grove, IL: InterVarsity Press, 1998.

_____. *Transforming Discipleship: Making Disciples a Few at a Time*. Downers Grove, IL: InterVarsity Press, 2003.

Orme, Brian. "Honest Talk." *Outreach 100*, October, 2013.

Pazmino, Robert W. *Foundational Issues in Christian Education*. Grand Rapids: Baker, 1997.

Putman, Jim. *Real Life Discipleship Training Manual*. Carol Stream, IL: NavPress, 2010.

Rainer, Thom S. *Autopsy of a Deceased Church*. Nashville, TN: Broadman amp; Holman, 2014.

_____. *High Expectations*. Nashville, TN: B & H Publishing, 1999.

Rainer, Thom, and Eric Geiger. *Simple Church*. Nashville: B amp; H Publishing Group, 2011.

Rainer, Thom, and Ed Stetzer. *Transformational Church*. Nashville: B amp; H Publishing Group, 2010.

Sanders, J Oswald. *Spiritual Maturity: Principles of Spiritual Growth for Every Believer (Commitment to Spiritual Growth)*. Chicago, IL: Moody Bible Institute, 1994.

Santrock, John W. *Life-span Development*. New York, NY: McGraw-Hill, 2011.

Smith, Gordon. *Called to Be Saints: An Invitation to Christian Maturity*. Downers Grove, IL: InterVarsity Press, 2014.

Stanley, Andy. *Visioneering.* Colorado Springs: Multnomah Books, 1999.

Stanley, Paul, and Robert Clinton. *Connecting: The Mentoring Relationships You Need to Succeed in Life.* Carol Stream, IL: NavPress, 1992.

Waggoner, Brad. *The Shape of Faith to Come: Spiritual Formation and the Future of Discipleship.* Nashville, TN: Broadman & Holman, 2008.

Whitesel, Bob. *Cure for the Common Church.* Indianapolis, IN: Wesleyan Publishing House, 2012.

Wilkins, Michael. *Following the Master: A Biblical Theology of Discipleship.* Grand Rapids, MI: Zondervan, 1992.

_____. *The NIV Application Commentary: Matthew.* Grand Rapids, MI: Zondervan, 2004.

Yount, William R. *Called to Teach: An Introduction to the Ministry of Teaching.* Nashville, TN: Broadman amp; Holman Publishers, 1999.

_____. *Created to Learn: A Christian Teacher's introduction to Educational Psychology.* Nashville, TN: B & H Publishing, 2010.

_____. *The Disciplers' Handbook.* Ft Worth: Self-published, 2006.

_____. *The Teaching Ministry of the Church.* Nashville, TN: B & H, 2008.

## Electronic Documents

Barna, George. "The State of Discipleship." Accessed December 6, 2015. https://www.barna.org/research/leaders-pastors/research-release/new-research-state-of-descipleship#.VmWt-ISfPfM.

Burton, Debra K. "A Multidimensional Assessment of the Impact of a Spiritual Growth Campaign (40 Day of Purpose) on Individual Spiritual Development." PHD diss., Liberty University, 2004. Accessed August 31, 2015. http://digitalcommons.liberty.edu/cgi/viewcontent.cgi?article=1184&context=doctoral.

Edge, Stephen. "Training Mentors to Assist Fellow Believers in Establishing Spiritual Disciplines Essential for Spiritual Growth and Maturity." DMin diss., Midwestern Baptist Theological Seminary, 2012. Accessed January 18, 2015. http://site.ebrary. com/lib/mbts/detail.action?docID=80098222.

Fairhope United Methodist Church. The Spiritual Growth Assessment Tool. Accessed September 28, 2015. https://fairhopechurch.files.wordpress.com/2009/04/spiritual-growth-assessment-tool.pdf.

Fillinger, Kent E. "The Church Size Matrix." Accessed December 16, 2015. http://christianstandard.com/2011/04/the-church-size-matrix-part-1.

Gallaty, Robby "Developing A Culture of Discipleship in Your Church." Accessed February 2, 2016. https://factsandtrends.net/2018/02/20/developing-a-culture-of-discipleship-in-your-church/

Gaultiere, Bill. "Spiritual Growth Survey." Soul Shepherding, 2003. Accessed September 3, 2015. http://www.soulshepherding.org/2003/07/spiritual-growth-survey.

Krejcir, Richard J. "The Style of Worship." Accessed October 30, 2015. http://www.discipleshiptools.org/apps/articles/?articleid=38860&columnid=156.

Laurie, Greg. "Discipleship Growth Review." Accessed October 1, 2015. http://www.camarillocommunitychurch.org/wp-content/uploads/2013/06/Discipleship-Growth-Review.pdf.

LifeWay Christian Resources. "Spiritual Gifts Survey, 2003." Accessed October 3, 2015. http://www.lifeway.com/lwc/files/lwcf_mycs_030526_spiritual_gifts_survey.pdf.

———. "Spiritual Growth Assessment Process". LifeWay Christian Resources, 2006. Accessed September 1, 2015. http://www.lifeway.com/lwc/files/lwcf_pdf_dsc_spiritual_growth_assessment.pdf.

Pritchard, Jimmy D. "Leading Believers to Spiritual Maturity Through the Examination and Application of Selected Principles for Spiritual Growth." DMin diss., Southwestern Baptist Theological Seminary, 2011. Accessed May 15, 2015. http://site.ebrary.com/lib/mbts/reader.action?docID=80070111.

Pulliam, Steven. "Pathways to Spiritual Growth." Central United Methodist Church, Fayetteville, AR. Accessed September 3, 2015. http://centraltolife.com/pathways.

Rittenhouse, Ralph. "Discipleship Growth Review." Camarillo Community Church, Camarillo, CA. 2010." Accessed September 3, 2015. http://www.camarillocommunitychurch. org/wp-content/uploads/2013/06/Discipleship-Growth-Review.pdf.

Spears, E. K. "Three Differences Between Traditional and Contemporary Worship." Accessed October 31, 2015. https:// healthychurchnetwork.wordpress.com/2012/07/25/three-dif-ferences-between-traditional-and-contemporary-worship/.

Stonemill Church. "Stonemill Church Spiritual Growth Assessment.' Accessed September 28, 2015. http://htps://www.surveymon-key.com/r/?sm=ROWZCrN2CsatEpC9VsGv6w%3D%3D.

Wright, Joe. "Fairhope UMC's Spiritual Growth Assessment Tool." Fairhope United Methodist Church, Louisville, Ohio, 2015. Accessed September 3, 2015. https://fairhopechurch.files. wordpress.com/2012/05/spiritual-growth-assessment-tool.pdf.

Willow Creek Church. "Reveal study." Accessed October 2, 2015. http://www.christiancoachingcenter.org/index.php/ russ-rainey/coachingchurch2/.

# ABOUT THE AUTHOR

$D$r. Randy Tompkins has been in Christian ministry since 1965, and has been a member of the church ministerial staff at ten churches in Oklahoma and Texas. He has also served on the staff of two denominational agencies and served as interim minister for six churches in Mississippi and Louisiana. Dr. Tompkins and Marlene were married in 1967. They have three daughters and sons-in-law, eight grandchildren, and three great-grandchildren.

Dr. Tompkins earned a Bachelor of Church Music, a Master of Religious Education, and a Doctor of Education Ministries. He earned the DEdMin at age sixty-nine. In 2006 Dr. Tompkins established Cornerstone Consultant Ministries in order to provide customized programs and resources for churches and religious organizations. He has had the privilege of leading training sessions, lectures, and customized programs in a majority of the states in the United States and Canada.

Dr. Tompkins holds to the belief the church of today should be biblically focused, spiritually minded, and practical in application. A church that is biblically based will develop the church's beliefs based on God's Word. A church that is spiritually minded will allow the Holy Spirit to guide the spiritual development of church members. A church that produces practical programs and events will view church members as individuals rather than a group.

—Rev. Bob Buckner

CPSIA information can be obtained
at www.ICGtesting.com
Printed in the USA
LVHW072242080621
689684LV00025B/2855